T0163710

the LEADERSHIP CORE

Praises for
the LEADERSHIP CORE

"Competencies get us to the door of leadership; character gets us to the 'other side' into new purpose-driven possibilities. The Leadership Core is a terrific resource to both lead in-character and on-purpose in today's challenging world!"

Kevin Cashman, Global Leader, CEO & Executive Development at Korn Kerry. Best-selling author of *Leadership from the Inside Out and The Pause Principle*

"*The Leadership Core* is an encyclopedia of leadership research and philosophy. In this comprehensive book, William Schrimer shares positive, effective and proven methods to help you become a successful leader. Each chapter is chock full of big learnings. Savor, absorb and apply."

David Cottrell, Author, *Monday Morning Leadership* and *Stop Drifting, Lift the Fog and Get Lucky … How to Become the Person You Want to Be.*

"William Schirmer's new book, *The Leadership Core*, covers a lot of ground. He introduces both timeless principles of leadership and provides new ideas you've not seen before. This is a good read for any student of leadership."

Mark Sanborn, President Sanborn & Associates, Inc. Author of *The Fred Factor* and *You Don't Need a Title to be a Leader*

"This is an insightful book which covers a number of leadership topics. *The Leadership Core* is very concise and full of interesting examples based on Schirmer's experience. Key questions are posed to help leaders and managers enhance their approach. It is an essential read for anyone involved in the process of leadership and provides practical guidance grounded in some theoretical perspectives."

Julie Hodges, Author of *Managing and Leading People Through Organizational Change*

"I found William Schirmer's book to be inviting and invigorating…No matter where you are in your leadership journey, The Leadership Core is for those looking to improve their leadership abilities. It is not just a list of 'what to do's,' but real-life experiences and remedies offered by someone who has 'been there' that will help your leadership skills improve and expand."

Tim Cruciani, CEO Citizens State Bank

"I found this to be a very easy read … We all can learn from this book as it does a great job of explaining how to structure your organization to win with good people that become good leaders!"

Brad Noel, EVP Republic Finance

the
LEADERSHIP
CORE

COMPETENCIES
for
SUCCESSFULLY
LEADING OTHERS

WILL SCHIRMER

NEW YORK

LONDON • NASHVILLE • MELBOURNE • VANCOUVER

the LEADERSHIP CORE
COMPETENCIES *for* SUCCESSFULLY LEADING OTHERS

© 2022 WILL SCHIRMER

All rights reserved. No portion of this book may be reproduced, stored in a retrieval system, or transmitted in any form or by any means—electronic, mechanical, photocopy, recording, scanning, or other—except for brief quotations in critical reviews or articles, without the prior written permission of the publisher.

Published in New York, New York, by Morgan James Publishing. Morgan James is a trademark of Morgan James, LLC. www.MorganJamesPublishing.com

Morgan James BOGO™

A **FREE** ebook edition is available for you or a friend with the purchase of this print book.

CLEARLY SIGN YOUR NAME ABOVE

Instructions to claim your free ebook edition:
1. Visit MorganJamesBOGO.com
2. Sign your name CLEARLY in the space above
3. Complete the form and submit a photo of this entire page
4. You or your friend can download the ebook to your preferred device

ISBN 978-1-63195-488-7 paperback
ISBN 978-1-63195-489-4 eBook
Library of Congress Control Number:
2021900457

Cover Design by:
Rachel Lopez
www.r2cdesign.com

Morgan James PUBLISHING

with...

Habitat for Humanity®
Peninsula and Greater Williamsburg

Morgan James is a proud partner of Habitat for Humanity Peninsula and Greater Williamsburg. Partners in building since 2006.

Get involved today! Visit
MorganJamesPublishing.com/giving-back

TABLE OF CONTENTS

ACKNOWLEDGMENTS

Many individuals served to inspire the content of this book, both directly and via research as my teams and I implemented leadership development programs and best practices for the organizations I've worked with. Daniel Hinsley, Keryn Rowland, Brad Noel, Tim Cruciani, Bob Schoofs, Garland Koch, Ken Brossman, Mark Rieland, Magali Delafosse, Paul Worachek, Mark Murtha, Gary Cohen and Butch Fuller were bosses, executive colleagues and consultants who left indelible impressions on me over the years with their integrity, wisdom, support, and kindness. I worked with a couple of them all too briefly, but real class never takes long to make its mark on me.

I've been fortunate enough to work with a number of excellent colleagues in HR, Learning & Development, and Talent Management over the years. These individuals were extremely supportive and hard-working teammates who also contributed to my leadership journey and learning. They include: Denise Johnson, Rick Klein, Crystal Everson, Erin Mueller, Casey Schmidt, Ann Sandstrom, Kaitlyn Dorn, Brent Wood, Eileen Girling, Joe Bembnister, Bob Benzinger, Areti Xioura, Joy Abogado, Rob Van Craenenbroeck, Lynne

Sumpter, Ben Wickerham, and Petr Gistinger. There are a number of others, including my HR colleagues at Heartland Financial, whom I was very fortunate to have called teammates.

In addition, I'd like to thank Morgan James Publishers, who gave me an opportunity to publish my inaugural book and provided valuable counsel to this first-time author. I appreciate you taking a chance on me. In addition, I'd like to thank my editor Angie Kiesling, who helped me to formulate a whole lot of thoughts and words into something that, in the end, I'm proud to represent as my work and hope others will find of value on their leadership journey.

A big thank you to my long-time friends Stephen Coskran and Peter Foley—although we don't talk as much as we should you help keep me grounded and sane when we do, during what has been a busy and eventful last couple of years! I am also, of course, very grateful for the love and support of both family and friends over the many years.

PREFACE

Like most of you, I have experienced successes and failures in work and life. I'm proud of some of my accomplishments and embarrassed by some of my shortcomings. I have an ego and a sense of pride, can be emotional at times, and my self-belief occasionally wanes. I'm not perfect, do not have all (or even most) of the answers, and at times wish I'd said—or done—something very different than I have. Sometimes I excel, and occasionally I disappoint myself. I also like to think I have a strong moral compass, a sincere commitment to do good, and a desire to leave a positive legacy for my family, friends, and coworkers. In many respects, this makes me normal.

If this sounds like you too, then welcome to the club. Most of us feel alone in analyzing our flaws and obsessing over our perceived weaknesses, but in truth we are not unique here. Just as you wonder whether you belong in the room, the person next to you is also contemplating whether they're worthy enough to be in the rare air of leadership.

We are all egotists, heroes, saints, and protagonists in varying degrees. An angel and a devil lurk in all of us, and our success in any pursuit in life entails our ability to successfully acknowledge and respond to this reality. Though I wish I'd done some things differently, I can't spend the time I have left absorbed in self-recrimination and regret, and neither can you. We can only be clever enough to learn the lessons that both success and failure provide. I don't pretend to be a great leader with all the answers, but over a career spent with other leaders who have behaved both admirably and very badly, some indelible impressions have left a mark on me. I hope they will do the same for you as you seek to chart your own path in leading others.

Leadership can be a (potentially rewarding) burden, and not many people are willing to bear it. It doesn't suit everyone's core talents either. This isn't because others are flawed, it's merely because exceptional performance is where talent and passion collide. If either basic leadership competencies or a sincere and strong interest in leading others for their—not our—benefit is absent, then a successful transition into leadership is unlikely to follow.

Leadership is also situational. In some cases, circumstances that play less to talents and leadership interests can transform into those that positively support both factors in others. I've run across and worked with those who subscribe to the "born leader" perspective—the idea that certain people possess some innate biological preconditions that destine them to good leadership, whatever the environment. I don't buy it. I think that's ego whispering in their ear, telling them that they were born exceptional. That's a comforting story we'd all like to believe, but countless stories demonstrate those "ordinary" others who worked hard at developing themselves, had a genuine interest in providing help and guidance to others, and encountered an environment that allowed them to flourish in a leadership role. If you have the selfless desire to lead and the circumstances allow you to use your core talents, then a couple of important facets of leadership success exist. All you have to do is continue your leadership development journey.

The core competencies of leadership are open to debate, and many capable theorists on leadership have put forward their own thoughts on this subject. There's no one perfect combination of leadership capabilities that is a panacea, and it's absolutely fair to say that the combination of leadership competencies that allow for success in some circumstances don't have the same positive impact in others. Nevertheless, I'm going to assert that a certain set of core leadership competencies are likely to benefit leaders in most environments. I certainly don't have all the answers, and perhaps only a part of our leadership exploration together will resonate with you. That's okay. Hopefully, you will understand your own leadership beliefs, competencies, and interests better along the way so you can apply them more effectively in practice.

Lee Kuan Yew, widely held to be the father of modern Singapore, said, "I do not yet know of a man who became a leader as a result of having undergone a leadership course." I believe this and think the same can be said for any facet of leadership study (including reading leadership books!). The key to becoming a leader isn't in learning about leadership but in applying the knowledge gained to good effect out in the "real world." Leadership is granted through action, not thought. We can discuss what actions are likely to result in effective leadership, and that is the aim of this book. I hope it provokes thought, challenges you, and leads you to a leadership place you are content with.

Section 1

CHARACTER IS THE
CORNERSTONE OF LEADERSHIP

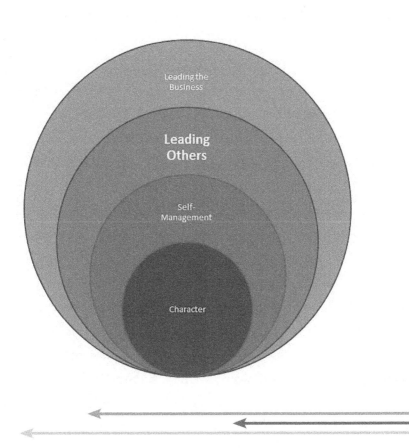

What is *character*? It's one of those uniquely human characteristics we define almost exclusively in our own minds. Is it the courage to stand up for what is right in the face of certain punishment? What about the ability to admit mistakes and our own human frailties? Or the humility to understand that the higher we climb, the deeper we must bow to others? We know it when we see it, and we notice where it's lacking. It isn't easy to put down on paper, though—to articulate with certainty what *character* really is. In my view, character contains several primary components, which are *integrity*, *accountability*, *humility*, *compassion*, and *responsibility*.

INTEGRITY

We need to start at the very beginning here, and that means discussing *integrity* first. Integrity is the absolute bedrock foundation upon which we build all other leadership competencies. If you attempt to build your house on the slippery slope of lying, cheating, and stealing, you'll be deservedly caught in a mudslide of recrimination. I have seen the careers of a number of people, including senior leaders, implode because they thought they were beyond reach or just chose to operate in their own self-interest at the expense of truth and integrity. What a shame. The good news is that commercial Darwinism catches these people at an increasing rate, and corruption is harder to hide in the age of social media, corporate social responsibility, and increased consumer transparency demands. Thank goodness for that.

So if you can't commit—completely commit—to the concept of integrity, put this book down now. The rest of the information in it won't do you any good if you lie, cheat, or steal in your role because no one will trust you. No one will build truly strong and productive relationships with you, and your influence will be terminally diminished. People can abide by most things, but not a liar, cheater, or thief. If you've already put a price on something that is priceless—as your reputation is one of the precious few items you carry with you throughout your life—then any success you may find is likely a fragile, fleeting illusion.

Now, this isn't to say that none of us has ever stumbled on the subject of integrity during our lifetimes. To deny this would be naïve and idealistic, ignoring the reality of human nature. There is a harsh reality about integrity that all grown-ups must face, however, and in business it's much more unforgiving: If you can't be trusted about something, then you can't be trusted about anything. When you are thirty years old, your boss doesn't have to forgive you like your mother did when you were ten. In the business world, the lack of truth, ethics, and the moral high road is much more evident. It can't be hidden by a lack of significant consequence to the business.

In most cases, integrity dies a death of a thousand cuts rather than one hammer blow. Time and bad moral judgment erode integrity to the point of collapse. We make a decision to contravene our own moral code and the concepts of truth and honesty. We may rationalize the decision as inconsequential and one unlikely to ever be called out. But *we* know. When we decide to compromise our integrity in this small way and discover that on this occasion it has no consequence, then we believe it's acceptable to repeat the process. But this time the lie—and its implications—are larger. When we escape the consequence yet again, we become emboldened and wonder why we made the additional effort of maintaining truth and the moral high ground in the first place. The best-case scenario is that it develops into a chasm between the leader we are and the leader we could have been; in the worst case scenario, the crack in our integrity foundation is terminal for our leadership career.

Integrity is an absolute measure, not one of degrees. Have you ever heard someone described as being "fairly honest"? I highly doubt it. We describe others as either honest or dishonest, trustworthy or untrustworthy, incorruptible or corrupt. This is because in the absence of one, we are the other. Someone once described integrity as a "pass/fail" ideal to me. I agree with them. You can't rate someone's integrity on a five-point Likert scale. You've got it, or you don't. If you don't, you don't get to play on the team.

Integrity is also important to the concepts of mutual accountability and delivering excellence. We can't forget that in team-oriented environments, we count on the persons around us possessing the level of integrity to ensure we deliver consistent service, follow through on commitments, and preserve the reputation of the group. When each person commits to carrying out their individual responsibilities with integrity, dedication, and quality, the "sweet spot" where these intersect is team excellence.

An integrity defect in our organization threatens us all. It's a cancer we have to promptly rid ourselves of. When you deal with lying, cheating, and stealing issues quickly and decisively—and publicly, where appropriate—you demonstrate commitment to integrity and to the severe consequences of violating business ethics. Staff gain respect because you backed up lofty talk about ethics with action and lived your moral code. No one is going to argue over—or sympathize with—the liar, thief, or cheat when due process was provided and decisive action was taken. People will shrug and move on with their day while their former coworker trudges off to the unemployment line to become some other organization's integrity problem.

When you fail to defend integrity as a leader and back up your organization's values, you signal to all that the moral bar has been lowered and the workplace culture has now been devalued. In defining "culture" for teams, someone once brilliantly said that it was "the worst performance or behavior that you'll accept." I like this definition immensely as it's simple and relatable for all. Your team members will see where the bar is that you've set.

People build culture, and by nature, people are an imperfect, unpredictable input. They lie, cheat, steal, self-destruct, disappoint, frustrate, and bewilder us. They also delightfully surprise, overachieve, inspire, motivate, move, support, and love us. If you want to build culture, you do it through the person sitting to the left of you and to the right. If you are at the very top of the organization there is no one beside you, then you must find checks and balances for the sake of your own leadership and the organization.

A story about Roman Emperor Marcus Aurelius speaks of a servant who regularly whispered in his ear, "You're only a man" to remind him of his mortality. It takes a great deal of courage and humility for CEOs and senior executives to remind themselves that they are not superior to others and that their role, more than any, exists to serve the needs of their people and their customers. Integrity starts at the very top. The rest of the organization takes its cues about what is right and what is wrong from everything senior executives say and do. Whatever level your leadership may operate at, remember that you're always on stage. There's always someone else looking to you, either as a role model, peer, or team member. If you compromise your integrity, someone will notice it sooner or later.

Organizations build a culture of integrity one employee and one leader at a time. The integrity transgressions of ground-level staff, having failed to be held to account by their supervisors or the organization's moral framework, send a message to all that lying, cheating, and stealing are options. They aren't. If you want to progress in your leadership career, make the right ethical choices and hold others accountable for making them as well.

I once ran across a very smart, charismatic man who put some "red dots" on a map of his company's operating area. Each dot represented someone he fired for making a poor integrity choice that jeopardized their own, and the company's, reputation. He explained how he was happy to help those who struggled with performance, but if they took matters into their own hands and crossed the line concerning matters of ethics, they had sealed their own fate. He held this discussion openly with his staff.

Any guess as to what happened afterward? You're right. He put up fewer "red dots" because as a senior leader, he set the tone for a high standard of integrity.

As an organization, be clear about your moral values. If you have a mission, vision, and values statement that's dusted off each year at annual appraisal time or paid lip service to for a few minutes when new teammates join, it's easy to tell. People's intrinsic "lie detectors" are sensitive in today's employment marketplace. Walk the walk, or don't talk the talk. Your employees pick up on everything you say and do. If your words are inconsistent with the values you espouse, you risk a loss of credibility that will drive low performance and engagement and drive high turnover.

I've held senior leaders to account who rationalized the unethical actions of their staff because they were good performers (usually because of the unethical acts they committed!). The first person you hold accountable sends a message to the rest that you are serious about the team's integrity and reputation and you won't compromise it. The high performers need to know that their productivity doesn't protect them from making wrong moral choices, and the low performers must realize that cheating their way to safety isn't an option. What results, in the long term, is a great team that not only does things right but does the right things.

———————▶

- *What are your core individual values?*
- *What do you do currently to set a positive example for integrity as a leader?*
- *Do you deal promptly with integrity issues as they arise or ignore them?*

- *Do you turn a blind eye to integrity issues coming from a "good performer" or do you consistently uphold your organization's moral values?*
- *How have you communicated the importance of integrity and the organization's values to your team members?*

HUMILITY

As we progress in our careers, gaining experience, specialist expertise, and a track record for success, our confidence is positively affected. We become used to being the "go-to" person—the one others count on to make things happen and get results. It feels good. Being in demand fulfils a basic human need for validation and significance. We not only crave others to tell us, and we also tell ourselves, how wonderful we are as we begin to believe "our own press." We become the smartest person in the room; the one who provides the answers rather than waits for them. We straddle the edge of the blade; that fine balance between self-confidence and arrogance, self-belief and narcissism. When you walk this narrow bridge there's risk of falling into a chasm of conceit.

The ego we see most commonly goes by a more casual definition: an unhealthy belief in our own importance. Arrogance. Self-centered ambition ... It's that petulant child inside every person, the one that chooses getting his or her own way over anything or anyone else. The need to be *better* than, *more* than, *recognized* for, far past any reasonable utility—that's ego. It's the sense of superiority and certainty that exceeds the bounds of confidence and talent. (Ryan Holiday, *Ego Is the Enemy*, p. 2)

The fall into arrogance and narcissism isn't uncommon, and it takes purposeful energy to guard against it. We've likely all encountered others like this; someone who honestly believes he or she is always the smartest one in the room, regardless of the subject discussed. They're an expert at everything; the frustrated vanguard of quality, performance, and intelligence who can't understand why others don't rise to the occasion to follow them and meet their needs.

There's significant danger in the ego that becomes a leviathan. The first is that the leader begins to self-isolate. Peers and subordinates can't stand to be in the room with someone who quite simply won't take advice or others' viewpoints into account. As a result, others view their time and talents as underutilized and wasted. They stop sharing their ideas and expertise. The word "team" becomes more and more meaningless as they play little part in affecting decisions but bear the brunt of the consequences. That doesn't feel good, regardless of the level at which employees operate. People simply vote with their feet and move away from environments that crush their self-esteem.

Periodically, a lack of humility masks itself in steadfast conviction to business philosophies and strategic plans that are out of touch with the capabilities and limitations of the organization. The failure to include staff closest to the end customer often leads to inaccurate assessments of the organization's ability and motivation to achieve goals. Expectations are set without a clear understanding of current realities and downstream effects on partners, customers, and employees. The people at ground level who are best equipped to save the organization from itself are ignored, and the avoidable iceberg is ploughed into.

The aggressive, grow-at-all-costs perspective masked as business ambition can hide a startling ignorance of the limitations of the business infrastructure, most importantly its personnel. The leaders around such executives may say nothing, as there is little point in arguing anymore. Instead of performing nearer to their potential, such organizations fracture under the weight of unrealistically ambitious plans.

An already-siloed organization can exacerbate the problem by allowing ego and pride amongst leaders to prevent real idea-sharing and collaboration. When that happens, those at the top had better be very right and perfectly accurate about the direction and capabilities of their organization—every single time. That, of course, is a bet that most of us wouldn't make. The egotist leader is blinded to the odds and the law of large numbers in arrogant decision making—meaning that the more decisions they make on their own, without the input of others who could have truly helped them, the more the quality of their decision-making reverts toward the mean amongst all people. At this point, raw intelligence doesn't matter if even the most genius among us sacrifices decisioning quality for the opportunity to take sole credit for successes.

Egotism and narcissism also distort reality regarding our own skills and limitations. Ryan Holiday discusses this in his book *Ego Is the Enemy*, a great read that I highly recommend. Egotism and self-love blind us to the gaps in our personal and professional skills. We cannot improve because we believe there's nothing to improve. Because we are already smarter, more skilled, more confident, and better in our rhetorical skills, we can't imagine taking significant steps to learn and grow because we exist instead to allow others to learn and grow from us. We are the wellspring of knowledge for them.

I believe in the executive coaching industry. It's necessary and beneficial. But even some executive coaches I've encountered readily admit that they often charge dearly to provide the same advice that an executive's own people have been attempting to provide for free, only to be stonewalled and dismissed. It's ironic that those at the top pay a complete stranger to at times tell them what their own staff has been saying all along. This happens because some executives can't fathom that good counsel could emanate from those who are already working with them. When a leader, at any level, truly believes that their need for continual learning is minimal they significantly stunt their own progression. They underperform against their potential and hold their organizations back. What a pity.

Wrapped up in all of these issues is temperament. For the egotist, it's acceptable to treat people badly as they simply aren't nearly as smart or valuable as the leader themselves. They just don't matter as much. These leaders treat others with disdain—viewing staff as a commodity in the quest to achieve commercial goals. Tempers flare regularly, and it's no surprise that others avoid challenging the leader, providing their ideas and suggestions, or interacting at all. The leader's phone calls go to voicemail. Because no one wants to provide bad news in the "kill the messenger culture" where they inevitably will be blamed, unpleasant surprises begin to mount for the organization. When this happens, the ability to deal effectively and proactively with problems decreases.

Staff members, who can more clearly see the unpleasant direction the team is heading in, begin to jump ship as there's no point in arguing with a leader who is always right. So they take their skills elsewhere, often beginning with the most talented employees. The lower performers stay, intensifying the problem of execution even further. Everyone suffers, including the leader, but they fail to see it. This is because the problems lie in everyone else's flaws rather than the leader's grand plan. Such a leader's office has plenty of mirrors, but none of them are for the purpose of thoughtful self-reflection.

Instead, take advice from the Chinese proverb that says, "Be like the bamboo—the higher you go, the deeper you bow." Remember to remain humble and bow deep, all the way to the most important level of people in your organization—those who deal with your customers. A little humility pays ... all the way to the bank.

---------->

- *Do you allow others to express their ideas and opinions, and do you truly listen to them?*
- *Do you provide the solution all the time to issues and problems? Are your ideas always the "best"?*
- *Do you accept feedback from others about issues, problems, and limitations that help you create realistic, well-informed goals?*
- *Do you reflect on your behavior and grow your own skills as a leader, or do you believe you already have all the expertise you need?*
- *Are you prone to emotional outbursts directed at your staff?*

<----------

ACCOUNTABILITY

This component of character is a big one. One organization I worked with taught me a lot about the power of personal accountability in gaining results and building a culture where staff understood ownership for their behavior and performance. The organization was clear about the value it placed on *accountability*, discussed it from the beginning of the interview process and in new employee induction, and reviewed it regularly throughout an employee's tenure. It built a culture of accountability where staff felt ownership for their work. This benefited all involved.

What is *accountability* exactly? First and foremost, it's a verb, not a noun. Accountability is expressed through action, not talk. Accountability, put simply, is "doing what you said you'd do, when and how you said you'd do it." David Cottrell, in *Monday Morning Choices* (p. 7) aptly describes this characteristic and the fact that it isn't what happens to us but how we choose to respond that determines our future plans, actions, and relationships. He acknowledged that the unexpected is going to happen to us, but we are in control of how to deal with it. We can be a victim, or realize that by taking control we can make strides toward greater successes.

Accountability is in the eye of the beholder. Whether we feel we've followed through on our commitments successfully is of little consequence. What matters is whether others feel that is the case. The recipient's opinion about our efforts is the only one that matters. When organizations have a constructive sense of mutual accountability, it propels them forward to consistent and strong results.

Accountability sharpens the saw. It focuses our efforts on being true to our word for our own sake, for those on our team and in our organization, and especially for the customer. When we do this and demonstrate full commitment to the result, we enhance performance. Because we take ownership of the good and bad and admit mistakes and our part in them, performance issues become a problem-solving exercise that is a normal part of doing business. The fingers point to uncover solutions, not cast blame. In such working environments, it becomes easier to lead and obtain results.

When a leader possesses true personal accountability and performance isn't realized, they look to themselves first rather than to others. Performance gaps become about what "I" as the leader could have done differently, or better, to ensure understanding of expectations, the maintenance of a culture of ownership, or proper follow-up to support results. As a leader, hold the mirror up first and examine your own shortcomings before you seek to examine those of others. If you underperform as a leader, your boss is going to look at your failings and yours alone. Why wouldn't you start there yourself?

Leaders never have the luxury of throwing their subordinates under the bus. You're ultimately responsible for your own behavior and results—and that of all those who report to you. Full stop. You can delegate ownership of tasks to individuals, but you own the performance outcome, without question. That's the price of being called "manager" and collecting the paycheck that goes with it. You only damage your credibility when you point the finger down, blaming your own subordinates for a lack of good results. Don't embarrass yourself and your organization by doing that.

Employees want to know what they're accountable for. They need to know well in advance, and also how you will measure their performance. When you provide that clarity for your team, accountability and results will increase. Provide your expectations to the team as a whole and to individual team members to ensure everyone understands their part in the team's success and the specific behaviors needed. Relay it in clear and simple terms, and confirm understanding *before* staff trod down the path to support the goals you've set.

Make sure the expectations you've set for some team members don't work against the goals of others and that a *line of sight* exists between their goals and the team's. Individual team members need to clearly see how their achievements support the aims of the team and organization. Remember that people are always watching you. Others will quickly observe you in action and judge whether your commitment to accountability is sincere or just hollow words. You can't just relay expectations. You have to live them through your actions and provide a role model for successful accountability.

Feedback also helps support accountability. Randy Pausch, in his moving lesson *The Last Lecture*, discussed feedback's role in increasing performance and demonstrating leadership care. He relayed a story from his youth in team sports, where his coach repeatedly chastised him and an assistant took him aside to remind him that this was a good thing. It's much better than the alternative; when you are making mistakes and you know it—and everyone else knows it—and no one is saying anything. Because that means others have already given up on you.

Randy reminded us that feedback, especially when it stings, is our critics' way of telling us that they still love us and care about our well-being. We also need to be very aware of intention when providing feedback. Our team members can readily tell whether the purpose of our feedback is to vent and make them feel bad about themselves or if it serves the more constructive purpose of helping them improve and achieve future results through positive performance coaching.

I've spoken to many leaders who neglect to build in regular one-on-one meetings as a normal way of discussing progress, obstacles, and future plans to support performance. Often, these same leaders are late with formal annual appraisals and the quality of their feedback using these processes is also poor. How unfortunate. They either fail to fully understand that their role is to obtain results through others' efforts, lack the interest in engaging with their people and coaching them, or don't possess the skills to hold feedback and coaching conversations.

If a leader can't properly focus on their people rather than process, then for their own benefit and the organization's they likely need to step aside. Leading people isn't for everyone. Build in the time to personally provide individual feedback and coaching to your people, or another employer will because you are going to start losing your staff.

Another structure that benefits leaders is the accountability loop. Henry Evans, in *Winning with Accountability*, stated that "there are no teams in ownership" (p. 66). We outlined this point earlier—that we may be accountable for results as a leader, but ownership of the tasks or actions is an individual phenomenon our team members experience. Remember to be clear in delegating individual responsibility for task completion—because if everyone 'owns' it then no one does, and you can expect underperformance.

Your level of active engagement with your staff is connected to the building of accountability loops. Absent managers don't build accountability. When your people know that you've built and maintained structures for follow-up and that you will have regular discussions regarding performance and behavior, you're going to increase individual accountability. Where expectations are well understood and individual tasks are clearly communicated, you can anticipate improved ownership and results. Everyone knows the objective and the part they must play to achieve it. This forms the accountability chain in teams which, when cascaded from level to level, is a powerful force for achievement.

Everyone is accountable to someone else, and is also the recipient of other accountable coworkers' efforts. We simultaneously hold ourselves and others to account through audits, regular one-on-one discussions, publishing of key performance indicators, performance appraisal/assessment activities, reward and recognition, and disciplinary processes.

Successful accountability is built from a broad and regular network of activities, not just a once- or twice-a-year use of formal performance appraisals. Accountable leaders avoid the reverse-engineering of performance appraisals to provide underperforming staff "acceptable" ratings and compensation increases because they want to avoid the uncomfortable conversations about needed improvements. They correlate performance appraisal ratings with organizational results and compensation changes to uncover weak links in accountability loops and strengthen them. They ensure that regular performance data is in others' hands, allowing them to adjust their behavior to achieve desired results. Importantly, such leaders match authority to responsibility and allow staff the freedom to make decisions—and bear the consequences for them—in a culture that doesn't crucify mistakes, but instead learns from them as part of the continual improvement process.

Leaders need to be aware of non-productive behaviors, in both themselves and their teams, that inhibit personal accountability cultures. These types of behaviors evidence an attitude that when things go wrong, the problem is "out there" and not lying within ourselves. They prevent us from looking in the mirror, blinding us to the fact that the root cause of issues might be very close to home.

On occasion these nonaccountability behaviors are more dramatic, while in most cases it's a subtle corrosion eating away from within. The authors of *The Oz Principle* (p. 12) remind us of this, indicating that nonaccountability creeps into organizations by coming unannounced as reasonable excuse, then escalating into the more aggressive blame-oriented accusation, and finally evolving into "the way we do things around here." They remind us that the price a culture pays for nonaccountability doesn't become clear until you see its antithesis: accountable people getting results.

This is an ample reminder that accountability, or lack thereof, permeates an organization and inhabits its culture through individual acts. Each act, and its consequence, sends a signal about the level of accountability in the environment. Observers will then form their conclusions about how high or low the organization is willing to go with the level of accountability it will accept.

- *What are you doing to ensure your own personal accountability remains high in the workplace?*

- *How are you building and maintaining an accountability culture on your team?*
- *Do you provide regular feedback to help your people remain accountable for behavior and results?*
- *How well do you set and communicate expectations to your team members today to assist with accountability?*
- *Do accountability loops exist on your team, including your use of follow-up, to help ensure accountability?*

<- —————————————————————

RESPONSIBILITY

The "responsible" person is sometimes maligned as predictable, boring, and uninteresting—as if it's a character flaw rather than a personal asset. This is very unfortunate. For me, the concept of *responsibility* contains the factors of self-discipline, conscientiousness, reliability, and sound judgment. Self-discipline involves taking care of the necessary, and at times unpleasant, tasks rather than putting them off because we are uninterested in them or they are unpleasant or routine.

Self-discipline is about control; being willing to dig in and face the hard challenge or unpleasant task rather than first do what is easy, safe, or more interesting. We do what we need to first so we can then do the things we want to. It's easy to recognize those who lack strong self-discipline; they simply operate the other way around, doing what pleases them first before what is necessary. The hard challenge or uninteresting task is put off, then rushed to completion.

Those who undertake the necessary tasks before those that are desired—and do them well—should be appreciated. As leaders, ironically we often "delegate" those tasks that we find uninteresting, repetitive, or routine to others so that we can make best and highest use of our own time. While this is a perfectly valid and logical business practice, we shouldn't forget to recognize those who perform such delegated tasks consistently well.

The responsible person makes a sincere, good faith effort to accomplish their aims. They dedicate themselves fully to achieving goals and overcome obstacles that stand between themselves and success. This is conscientiousness at work; not doing the job just to say that it's done, but that it's been done to the best of their ability based on proper focus and effort. The conscientious person doesn't just "go through the motions." They demonstrate true attention, whether the task is challenging or not and interests them or not.

People who brighten others' lives in the course of performing routine, ordinary tasks are indeed extraordinary and should be cherished for their efforts. They are the engine of every successful operation, and we need to celebrate and retain them. Find the person who wants to do everything that they do well and you have a diamond in the rough, as long as their talent matches their ambition. Give me one of these individuals any day, and I will work to polish them rather than the individual who "talks a good game," looks good in an interview, and feels entitled to rewards before they put in the hard work to prove their worth.

Responsible people are also reliable. This is the consistent effort and results that help leaders sleep well at night. Knowing that once an initiative is delegated we can predict consistent, quality results through others is very valuable to any leader. We all know the person who "just gets it done"— someone you can count on to do a good job regardless of the circumstances or challenges, and will guard the team's reputation carefully through their consistent results.

The responsible person demonstrates reasonable judgment. Their considered, thoughtful approach to decision-making helps the organization thrive. These individuals are a key asset to organizations and can be taught to use techniques to gather and analyze information, apply risk-management methodologies, and supercharge their critical thinking and judgment skills even further.

What elements, fundamentally, account for "sound" judgment? One element is sensitivity to, and emotional awareness of, the downstream effects on people. Leaders obtain results through the work of others. And good leaders are aware of the effects of their words, behavior, and decisions on others. They think ahead, considering the consequences of their decisions on people's emotions, productivity, engagement, and retention. Such leaders feel the weight of decisions, understanding that the process of coming to conclusions affects their most important asset in the organization: people. When a leader acts with both mind and heart in weighing decisions, he or she sends the message that people matter, and not just because of their work productivity.

The use of information, logic, and process (i.e., risk management) to make decisions also hones judgment. Of course, it isn't just about the fact that we have information, or apply a rational approach, as data sources can be suspect and our logic flawed. But the act of gathering information, assessing its validity, and applying it appropriately to make decisions helps. When we apply a rational approach using information, the quality of our outcomes increases.

As leaders, we shouldn't become islands unto ourselves as we use our judgment to make decisions. The leader who is humble enough to ask for others' opinions demonstrates even better judgment, as they are using more of the knowledge resources at their disposal to make informed decisions.

Subjecting important decisions to public scrutiny, even if opinions vary, allows you to test the quality of the information you are using to make them and the logic you are applying to determine action. If your judgment can't weather this examination then you have a problem.

The responsible leader is self-disciplined in how they approach their duties and obligations to themselves, their teams, and the organization, and is conscientious in applying their best efforts to carry out their duties and meet expectations. They also demonstrate reliability; a quality we also ask from every team member so we can predict behaviors and outcomes more effectively. Last, the sound judgment applied to make decisions is a function of the responsible leader, who is sensitive to their own biases and emotional triggers, considers the tangible and intangible outcomes of their actions, and applies information, logic, and process to make important decisions.

- *Do you demonstrate self-discipline, doing the hard, unpleasant, or uninteresting things that are necessary, or do you put them off to pursue your own interests?*
- *Are you conscientious, dedicating your full effort and attention to all tasks to produce your best work?*
- *Do you use sound judgment, weighing data and information, as well as the ideas and opinions of others, to arrive at well-considered decisions?*
- *Would others consider you reliable—someone who delivers consistent, quality work on time to meet expectations?*
- *What do you do today on your team to uphold a culture of responsible behavior?*

COMPASSION

The ability to demonstrate care, kindness, and concern for the welfare of others is not only a desirable human quality but also a trait that enhances leadership effectiveness. *Compassion* is a core necessity to building and maintaining strong relationships with others, and where it is lacking it stands out as a negative. Basic human decency entails the ability to show compassion for others when it's required, and employees are sensitive to the manner in which leaders deal with the welfare and misfortunes of their people.

Leaders are always "on stage," and our actions send a message about our priorities, the kind of culture we want to build and maintain, and how others will likely be treated if similar situations arise in the future. In the people versus profits debate, the presence or absence of compassion signals which side of the fence our leadership falls on. If staff members come to know that they are always a secondary priority for you, they in turn will deprioritize your leadership and the organization. Decreases in engagement and productivity—and increases in employee relations issues and turnover—will inevitably occur.

The old stereotype of the command-and-control leader, dispassionately directing others with only a focus on logic, facts, and "the bottom line" has faded. Today's workforce demands a more balanced approach that demonstrates care and concern for team members, customers, and the communities in which our businesses operate. If others don't receive a compassionate leadership approach from us, they'll likely seek it out down the road at our competitor's business as the human need to be appreciated, validated, and approached with empathy is fundamental.

This doesn't mean we sacrifice making smart and tough commercial decisions just to make our people feel better about themselves. It does mean that our people's welfare is a factor in the equation when the tough decisions are made, however, and the basic approach to dealing with others is thoughtful and kind. It's common sense for most leaders but is a foreign concept lost on a few others.

Compassion is demonstrated in both word and action. It's evidenced when we practice empathy, identifying with the situations others are in and the emotions they're going through. When we can sincerely envision others' pain, distress, and discomfort, we can respond in an appropriate way that demonstrates care and concern. Do we truly understand how it *feels* to experience: the loss of a loved one; breakup of a marriage/relationship; serious illness; household move; job loss; making a serious mistake; failure; major interpersonal conflict; and serious embarrassment and regret? How can we provide genuine support for others experiencing these issues? In more joyful times, such as marriage, graduation, anniversaries, birthdays, and personal or professional accomplishments, do we acknowledge our people and help them celebrate, adding to the good feeling, or do we ignore the joyful times and detract from the well of positivity?

To demonstrate compassion, you have to get out of your own head and your office and take interest in your people. Walk around and make conversation with them. Ask them how the weekend went and what exciting plans they may have for the future. It's not wasted time. You're humanizing yourself and building relationships. You're also demonstrating a sincere interest in others that can only positively impact engagement, morale, productivity, and retention in the long run. The return on investment of your time here is huge. It's good business.

I once worked with an executive in a small company who was an accountant by trade and had extraordinary interpersonal skills. He made conscious efforts to "make the rounds" and personally see how people were doing. He engaged them, ate lunch in the canteen with them, and took every opportunity to get to know them better and form real human connections. He was truly curious about the lives of his workforce, and he built up very positive relationships with his people. They, in turn, worked hard for this executive, dug deep in difficult times to help the organization, and were considerate to the boss and to each other. They did so because of the loyalty he engendered and the respect he gave. The goodwill came back to him in droves.

Another aspect of compassion is forgiveness. Certain acts may simply not be forgivable in business—as lying, cheating, and stealing lie beyond the pale—and leaders need to decisively root out such individuals from their teams. But in all other things, we can choose whether to respond with forgiveness or wrath when behavior or performance issues arise. The compassionate leader assigns benign intent to circumstances until proven otherwise. It allows us to deal with tough situations and difficult conversations in a considerate way. The end result may still be negative consequences for others, but when we handle these situations well, they are taken care of with the thoughtfulness that prevents unnecessary conflict and ill-feeling.

You also get to choose whether the price of mistakes and underperformance is learning or loss. Is this mistake a pivotal moment where our team member can take away an important lesson that will help them operate better in future? I once heard about an employee who made a large mistake with a client that cost his employer millions in revenue. Called in to the boss's office shortly afterward, he expected to be fired. As the conversation with the boss unfolded, the boss concluded by saying, "Fire you? Why would I fire you? I just spent millions training you!" This demonstrates an extraordinary approach where this leader weighed whether they could find a better employee elsewhere, or if the expensive learning lesson and loyalty they could gain via forgiveness would pay a dividend in the long run. Now is the story true? I don't know, but the lesson it teaches is certainly valuable.

Leaders have to weigh such considerations, and certainly, forgiveness in all circumstances isn't the appropriate path. Team members may intentionally misbehave and put their teammates' safety and well-being at risk. They may sabotage their own or the team's performance and undermine the company's results. In such cases the right path usually means they can't remain on the team. There's a fundamental difference between performance and behavior issues that do not arise from malicious intent and those that do.

Leaders have a choice. They can be caring, considerate, and kind in what they say and do with all who they encounter, or they can be thoughtless, ignorant of feelings, and at times downright mean-spirited. We're all going to leave a legacy that will far outlive our careers. Acting with compassion may just help ensure it is a positive one for both you and others long after you're gone.

- *What do you do today to demonstrate care and concern for your team members?*
- *Do you take your people's welfare into account when making decisions that affect them?*
- *Do you respond with empathy when your people have problems in/outside of work, or important events and accomplishments in their lives?*
- *Are you tolerant of mistakes and use them as learning opportunities, or are you intolerant of errors?*
- *What do you do today to learn more about your people and take an interest in them?*

Section 2

MOTIVATING

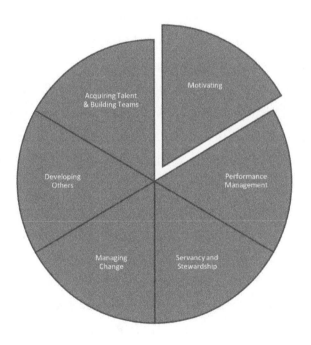

Desire. Determination. Passion. Hunger. Inspiration. Motivation has many names. The term often conjures some "Braveheart" type of speech, where the leader is charismatically addressing the group to summon courage to do battle for a noble cause. Perhaps you visualize the coach giving a rousing speech to inspire your favorite sports team to an improbable comeback victory. These visions are often intimidating for managers not blessed with great oratory skills—those who perceive themselves as lacking presence.

The modern-day business reality, however, isn't quite as dramatic as in the movies, sports, or on the political stage. In our team environments at work, we deal with "normal" people and don't have to motivate through grandiose gestures or speeches. Motivation happens in more subtle ways, through the individual and in groups, and is less about direct inspiration than it is about providing an atmosphere that satisfies your team members' emotional needs.

Former U.S. Navy Captain Michael Abrashoff knew this fact too. His wonderful book *It's Your Ship* relayed how his leadership approach allowed his crew to turn a poorly performing US Navy ship into a record-achiever. He stated that "as I saw it, my job was to create the climate that enabled people to unleash their potential. Given the right environment, there are few limits to what people can achieve" (p. 29). Abrashoff's crew responded to the cultural change he enabled, and indeed reached greatness. They did so not because he was the captain. The opportunity to satisfy psychological desires, which existed because of the environment Abrashoff built, fueled their accomplishments. He built it one action, one conversation, one decision at a time—because that is how solid foundations for repeatable success are created.

In our own way, we each are the captain of our ships. While yours or mine might be smaller than a Navy battle cruiser, all of us still help determine whether our team is inspired to reach our ultimate port of call: achievement.

As leaders, we help chart the course and scan the horizon for danger. We encourage our crew to keep moving toward the destination through emotional appeal. We allow the navigator and the rest of the team members to leverage their unique talents in an environment that lets them also make some of the decisions. In this way, each part of the ship has someone who feels personally responsible for their contribution in getting it to an appealing destination.

Why do we care about "motivation" as leaders in the modern workplace? Shouldn't our people nowadays (if we hire the "right" ones) come with their own drive to achieve, whatever the goal? As leaders we should care more, not less, than ever before about stoking high-performance desire in our people.

> Employees' attitudes and especially their motivation—or overall enthusiasm for doing their work well—are a growing concern for all managers ... There are two reasons for this: 1) Today's fast-changing, challenging work environment is more likely to create negative feelings, such as stress and frustration, and therefore poses a constant threat to healthy work attitudes. 2) The need for creative problem-solving and rapid adjustment to change means that employees must be more self-motivated than ever before. Regimented, obedient employees do not succeed in today's challenging environment. Managers depend on employee initiative, enthusiasm, and commitment more than ever before. (Hiam, *Motivational Management*, p. 7)

The workplace of a century ago required workers' hands and feet, not their hearts and minds. Heavily labor-based in nature, leaders looked for workers with strong backs and the ability to produce quantity of output under less than ideal physical working conditions. "Scientific" theories of labor caused task analysis to break down work into small parts, with specialized team members performing one narrow duty that made work repetitive and menial.

The desire for workers to add value by sharing opinions and be emotionally driven to achieve never entered into the equation. Today, if leaders want to leverage hands and feet, they *must* capture hearts and minds to build and sustain performance. It's at the heart of the performance equation, and this is why motivation is an important leadership subject we must explore. With motivation, the quality and source of it—not quantity—is the difference maker. It isn't just about harvesting any feeling that works to get the job done through others. It's about leveraging emotions that are positive, selfless, and in harmony with the team's shared goals. It might sound complicated, but it's not as daunting as it seems.

There's debate about whether a leader even acts to motivate directly or whether motivation is only internal to individuals by its very nature. The argument seems semantic to me. Whether as a leader you directly inspire, or do so indirectly by creating an environment in which team members tap into something within themselves, isn't the net effect is the same? Yes and no. The short-term effect may be identical, as both can drive staff to meet performance goals. The difference lies in long-term sustainability of different motivational tacts.

Think of when fear and threat of punishment motivated you in the past. They may have worked in the short term, but what damage did they cause? Stress? Absenteeism? Morale and engagement declines? A job switch? Negative feelings toward your boss and the company? Loss of respect? The possible list is long. No one likes the sinking feeling of their job being constantly under threat—being one mistake or bad performance away from the unemployment line. In such cases, team members simply take their skills elsewhere. Contrast that with a time you felt highly motivated at work. It came from a more positive place, one that likely aligned well with your personal drivers, values, and aspirations. Was it recognition? Appreciation? Inclusion? Personal growth? Purpose? Achievement? These are deeply held emotions that individuals and their leaders can leverage time and time again to satisfy mutual needs. That's the strong oak of motivation that weathers well.

INTERNAL VERSUS EXTERNAL MOTIVATORS

A fundamental difference exists between intrinsic, or internal, motivations and external ones. The latter are provided as an end result of accomplishing the work. These are the things that must be given to individuals for desire to be satisfied. They can also be withheld. Bonuses, prizes, awards, promotions, and recognition are external motivators. The satisfaction of these types of motivators doesn't lie within the work itself but in accomplishing the work to gain some reward. Work efforts that don't result in external motivators being satisfied sometimes leave us bitter and unfulfilled.

Intrinsic motivators are those that we don't have to wait on or depend on anyone else for, because they're provided as an inherent part of doing the work itself. Performing the task itself satisfies the internal driver and, unless the job is taken away or significantly changed, the motivation to achieve remains steady. Achievement, personal growth, purpose, significance, and professional pride are examples of intrinsic motivators.

Likely, we view external motivators as those that the manager directly influences and internal motivators as indirectly shaped by leaders. Those that speak of indirect leadership influence contend that leaders only create the circumstances in which individuals access their internal motivations, rather than directly acting as the catalyst by which those desires are fulfilled. Lydia Banks, in *Motivation in the Workplace*, argues that "as a manager, you want to develop and encourage good employee performance, and good performance comes from strong employee motivation. But managers can't *motivate* employees. Motivation is an internal state, like emotions and attitudes, that only the individual can control. Managers can, however, create a workplace environment that will inspire and support strong motivation on the part of employees" (p. 7).

One prominent school of thought, then, is that internal motivators are more powerful and sustainable than external motivators and that a leader's role is merely to cultivate an atmosphere in which people can tap into their intrinsic motivations. Passions that run through our veins run deep, and withstand the adversity and change that inevitably come to pass in our lives. Leveraging these desires is more sustainable than the short-game of providing external incentives for performance. When you use the latter, you need to keep feeding the machine to receive the desired outcomes, and as people build up a tolerance to the level of reward you provide, you have to give more and more to receive the same level of performance in the future. This is the epitome of the law of diminishing returns.

If you provide all of the motivation and it does not come from within the person, your team members are responding only because that is what they need to do to receive the short-term benefit they perceive as valuable. That's precisely why motivation can appear as a zero-sum game. The more external motivation is employed the less internal motivation can be leveraged. Paul Marciano, in *Carrots and Sticks Don't Work*, says that "… the more emphasis put on the extrinsic reward, the less internal motivation an employee feels toward the task. Reward and recognition programs actually diminish the perceived value of the task to the employee; psychologically the employee is doing the task not because it is important but because he or she can benefit from it materially" (p. 32). Overreliance on external motivators, particularly in the form of compensation and special award programs, may be counterproductive for the long-term motivational health of an organization.

External motivators are a commodity; they are the easily repeatable aspects of the employment relationship that any company, with enough money, can provide. Base pay, bonuses, or benefits? Anyone with a higher offer or better deal down the road can draw your people away. Promotions, job title, or recognition? As an employee, you might receive them in the future, or you might not. There are lots of risks around dependence on external motivators, as they may never come to pass despite your best efforts. Internal motivators, on the other hand, remain to some extent whether or not the goal was achieved. In the long-term, the ability to fulfill at least part of your team member's work aspirations provides the emotional fuel to keep going in the face of performance setbacks. Contrast that with the disappointed face of the person expecting the bonus that never came, and you will see a significant difference in sustained individual motivation to perform in the future.

- *What drives you more: internal motivators or external rewards?*
- *What do you rely on to motivate your people primarily: internal or external motivators?*
- *Do you know what motivates your individual team members more: internal or external motivators?*

INDIVIDUAL VERSUS COLLECTIVE MOTIVATORS

Because each of our people has drives and aspirations that are different from their teammates, we must appreciate and adapt to them to move the team toward our goals. We've got to relate the aspirations of our people to the goals of the team and organization, aligning individual talent to the environment in a way that helps the work experience become even more rewarding. When team members take meaning and intrinsic reward from their work, grow personally and professionally, and leverage their talents to be successful, synergy arises between the job and personal drivers that results in high motivation. It's precisely because of what Kenneth Thomas, in *Intrinsic Motivation at Work*, calls "this diversity of passion" (p. 52) that leaders should try to match tasks to individual interests and allow people to participate in initiatives that align with both their skills and their individual drives.

You can't identify and leverage the unique drives—particularly the powerful intrinsic motivators—of individuals on your team if you don't get to know them. Leadership is a relational endeavor. To operate effectively, you need to forge ties with your people and learn about their talents and dreams. People expect you to learn about both if you're to be useful to them, just as you expect that they'll be useful to the team's objectives. Learning about and aligning individual talent and passion to tasks is not only good leadership, it's good business. Harter and Wagner, in *12: The Elements of Great Managing*, reference a study that found that organizations fully leveraging the natural talents of their staff had annual employee engagement increases of 33 percent, which equated to bottom-line productivity increases of $5.4 million on average (p. 42). Increases in performance are a part of a virtuous motivation circle, along with higher employee engagement and retention, that benefits organizations and teams.

While responding to individual motivators is important, leadership has to balance this with the need to forge shared purpose that is also motivational for all. Because leaders are tasked with reaching common team goals, a shared purpose with broad appeal should be identified and communicated. This is also important to team culture and identity, which is best formed around purpose. From this, leaders can then align individual drives with the shared purpose so that team members understand that they can also satisfy their motivations by supporting the team's aims. The priority in the end, however, is *shared purpose*. Where individuals can support shared purpose through their performance and behavior, an effective team results. When individuals cannot align themselves to the reason the team exists it detracts from group synergy and performance, at times to the degree where a leader must decide whether to keep them on the team.

---------------→

- *What are your own individual motivators?*
- *Do you know what each of your team member's motivators are and how they differ?*
- *How do you use your team members' individual motivators to help your team achieve its goals?*

←---------------

MONEY AS MOTIVATOR

Money is the ultimate workplace commodity. Everyone—except those seeking volunteer workers—offers it. There's nothing unique about money except that some employers may offer more of it than others. It doesn't buy better relationships with coworkers, a better boss, or increased meaning from performing the work itself. It doesn't make mundane tasks more interesting or the mission of the company more appealing. It's simply a means to an end, rather than the end itself. It cannot purchase meaning.

Money is an external motivator. Like other external motivators, it's provided in the hopes of sustaining motivation to keep doing the work, or in the case of performance incentives provided at the end of a work period as a reward. Like other external motivators, it often has limited usefulness above a certain point. As long as we feel competitively compensated, providing more money doesn't adequately compensate for the problems of the job itself or other shortcomings of our work experience. It's just a temporary dressing on a wound that won't heal.

We all have either witnessed someone in, or personally experienced, a job where no amount of money would lead to a return to a former employer. While the absence of what we believe is adequate pay can demotivate us, there is a point above which more does little to motivate us, particularly in light of fundamental issues with our work experience. Yet employer after employer pays above market rates and dangles heavy bonuses and retention incentives in front of their people to literally overcompensate for deficits in their employees' work experience. There is also likely to be little proof of positive ROI that they can point to as a result of doing so.

Once spent, money fades into memory rather quickly and there's a decreasing return on the investment for the team. The first time that bonus is achieved, the feeling is sweet, albeit temporary. The money is used somehow, likely in ways few of us remember in the long term. And the next time the incentive is dangled in front of team members, it takes more of it and/or the ability to earn it more often to elicit a similar level of motivation as in past. As counterintuitive as it may seem, money is simply a bad long-term investment in the motivation and retention of people, particularly if it's the primary tool in your leadership toolbox. If you only have a hammer, then everything looks like a nail. The problem with this? Once you drive the nail home, you can't keep pulling it out and doing it again to have the same effect.

Generally, a company's desperate effort to retain an employee who has quit by throwing more money at them proves unsuccessful. That's because the team member's primary motivation to leave in the first place is rarely about money (although likely they received more of it as a byproduct of their job search) and the employee wonders about the company's sincerity and timing of its effort. They're likely to think: *Oh, NOW you want to tell me that I'm valuable and appreciated by giving me more money. No thanks! I already got that down the road, as well as satisfying the other parts of my work experience that were missing here.* A steadfast reliance on money as the main tool of motivation is a crutch that denies a leader's responsibility and ability to use other forms of motivation to achieve objectives.

> When leaders and their employees attribute their workplace dissatisfaction to money or external factors, it sets up a series of erroneous assumptions and detrimental actions. First, even though people need and want money and external rewards, believing those will make them happy distracts them from what actually does make them happy. Second, it lets leaders, who typically don't have direct control over pay raises and rewards, off the motivational hook. They throw their arms up in a leadership mea culpa and declare there's nothing they can do. (Susan Fowler, *Why Motivating People Doesn't Work … and What Does*, p. 129)

In our discussion of motivation, we will explore several primary motivators that can help build sustainable performance, engagement, and morale on your team. None of these factors are externally focused. These diverse factors, whether leveraged directly or indirectly to inspire team members, can be employed by any leader. Precisely *because* these factors don't rely on great oratory skills or personal presence and are simple in concept, they can be applied by either the newest of managers or the most experienced of executives.

- *How heavily do you rely on money as a motivator for your team members?*

- *How many of your team members have described money as one of their top two motivators?*
- *Have you ever attempted to "throw money at the problem" in motivating and retaining a staff member, rather than try to fix the core problem with their experience in the workplace?*

PURPOSE, MEANING, AND SIGNIFICANCE

If you want to inspire people, give them a reason to stand behind. It can't just be any reason; it has to be a reason that stokes and satisfies an internal desire. Carrots and sticks really don't work in moving people to start walking the long road to success, to keep feet moving over or around obstacles, and to stay on the path. Few people fail to begin the journey when a noble cause lies behind it. As we discussed earlier, motivators can be individual and collective, and in the case of purpose, it's no different. In providing vision, it must be both, as the most effective purposes satisfy the desires of both the group and the individuals within it. The reason for this is simple: Dig beneath the surface and you'll find that people never really work for you; they work for themselves. If you're perceptive enough to align them with collective purpose, however, they will also work for the good of the team.

No one sees their purpose as working for you. It isn't what brings meaning to their jobs and their lives. Whatever it may be, that meaning must be present though. "The reality is simple: people care less about working for a company than they care about working for a compelling purpose. **Meaning precedes motivation.** Our purpose answers the most fundamental question, 'Why do we do what we do?' Without a compelling purpose, without something bigger than ourselves to focus on, your team members just put in their time.

A team without purpose is a team without passion" (Colan, *Engaging the Hearts and Minds of All Your Employees*, p. 110).

We all may have been in a role, or managed someone in a role, where a sense of meaninglessness prevailed. Unable to draw more significance from the work other than filling the hours of the day and bringing home a paycheck, the job becomes torturous over time. We suffer until we can escape to another career opportunity that will help us make better sense of our existence. Discretionary effort simply doesn't flourish in a directionless environment.

Providing purpose is about tapping into emotional energy. We're all passionate about *something*. While that something is different for each of us, we can also identify some purposes that we can align ourselves to more than others. For instance, if you're passionate about creating great customer service experiences and helping others in need, you can heartily support a team purpose to deliver service excellence to the stakeholders it serves. When faced with obstacles, difficulty, setbacks, or outright failures, we persevere and remain focused on a vision of the future that we find personally exciting.

Kenneth Thomas, in *Intrinsic Motivation at Work,* stated that "fortunately, organizations' needs for committed, purposeful work fit an intense human need for purpose. It is the purpose aspect of the new work that most engages and stirs our passions ... Much of the color of our lives comes from the drama, challenge, struggle—and it is hoped the triumph—of handling the uncertainties involved in accomplishing those purposes" (pp. 20-21). While we cannot manufacture more time or attention in our lives, we can generate the passion that helps make the days we fill more meaningful and successful.

A passionate life, at work or at home, is one well-lived. Passion is like a solar generator. We just need to ensure that our team members each face the sun. The role of leadership, then, is to find the direction to face each of our people in so they can capture and then release emotional energy. As leaders, we've got to orient each person in a slightly different way, using those individual motivators, to help them align their passion with team vision.

You don't have to be highly visionary or inspirational to accomplish this. Most of us aren't. Our team members will instead draw their own inspiration because a primary factor that enhances employee motivation is merely a manager with a vision. It doesn't have to be grand, and it doesn't have to always stir some deep emotional reaction in us. The purpose you set for your team just needs to be clear, easy to understand, and something that goes beyond the bounds of commercial success for the organization. Just define a good reason the team exists (a "bigger" purpose) and explain it well.

David Novak, in *Taking People with You*, provides an example: "The Starbucks vision statement, for example, isn't anything as obvious as 'to make great coffee'; it's 'to inspire and nurture the human spirit, one person, one cup, and one neighborhood at a time'" (p. 115). With a little forethought, you can create your own simple statement that transcends operational success and has broad appeal.

You can further enhance purpose through storytelling. If you want to make purpose clear, tell the story of the customer, client business, or community that was meaningfully impacted through the team's efforts. Find a story that makes people laugh, cry, or feel pride. The best stories tap into team members' emotions to drive the point home that what they do is significant; that they make a positive difference that wouldn't be the same without them. Tell those success stories, and your people will keep coming back in to work, day after day, to create more of them.

We create and communicate purpose because we need to harness employee talents—and passion unleashes talent. We do it not only for this reason but also because employees demand it. In the absence of purpose, team members can't make meaningful choices about how to undertake their work. Instead, the day just becomes about "doing." Purpose places efforts in context and allows us to contribute to the vision in our own unique fashion. In today's workforce, purpose is particularly crucial.

> Researchers on generational differences note that younger workers (Generation Xers and millennials) are especially likely to demand meaningful work—and to leave if they do not find the work meaningful. These younger workers also want more freedom to work in their own style, finding their own ways of accomplishing a task purpose. So today's workforce and the new work combine to produce a growing demand for meaningful work. This demand is becoming a powerful force in the new job market. (Thomas, *Intrinsic Motivation at Work*, p. 22)

People want to choose how to accomplish purpose. If we tell our people exactly how to undertake every detail of their work, no matter how inherently inspired they are with purpose, their motivation will soon fade because we are holding talent back and detracting from meaningfulness. We've tapped into passion but not allowed that passion to unleash talent. You've captured hearts and minds, only to have your people employ just their hands and feet. In that case, why would they choose to remain on your team? People want to be a navigator in the process, not just a passenger.

Do not underestimate the importance of creating and communicating a clear and compelling purpose to your team. Whether you're building a new team or inheriting one, don't assume that your people already know and understand collective purpose. One of the greatest mistakes leaders make is to take on a new job and just start "doing" without defining, either for themselves or their people, to what higher purpose the team's work is intended to effect. They haven't answered the fundamental questions that they and their people ask about their work experience: "Why am I here?"

"What difference do I make?" "Why should I be motivated to contribute?" "Why should I remain?"

A job isn't just a job, of course, which is why people move employers periodically and leadership matters so much to the experience of our team members. Start your leadership by giving people a reason to come in and do their work well each day and you'll find the rest of your efforts will flow with the current rather than against it. Maintain that sense of significance by devoting attention to your people. Interacting one-on-one with your people signals that they are not just a cog in the machine. It shows them that they matter to the group and to the success of purpose.

- *Have you clearly explained your team's purpose to the individuals within it?*
- *Do you know what meaning each of your people draw from their work?*
- *Do you periodically discuss purpose and help team members refocus on it?*
- *Have you defined the purpose of your own leadership?*

EMPOWERMENT, TRUST, AND AUTONOMY

Empowerment is a basic motivational need. It revolves around freedom of choice, trust, engendering commitment and accountability, and people's ability to employ their unique talents. After we've set collective purpose and learned about our individual team members—including their ambitions, concerns, talents, frustrations, and experience—we can increase our chances of reaching team goals by allowing our people discretion in how to accomplish them. We *empower* them to do so. While empowerment may mean something a bit different to each one of your people, some basic concepts around it are universal.

Empowerment is just a popular expression for: 1) providing people the resources and latitude they need to accomplish their work, 2) allowing people to learn through mistakes and experience as a result of their own decisions, and 3) eliminating barriers to success. All it requires is genuine interest in making these resources available to your people and the humility to understand that you don't have all the knowledge, answers, or ability alone needed to accomplish team purpose. You must understand that this means trading some of the direct power you hold as a leader for an increase in the team's drive to accomplish goals and their engagement in team purpose.

Power is distributed to increase the potential of achievement. It's a fallacy that the more a leader distributes his or her power, the less they have. It's much closer to the truth to say that power multiplies as you distribute it instead of dividing. A leader's power doesn't decrease, it just becomes more indirect. Power is a seedling waiting for the right conditions to sprout up. You're simply providing power a more fertile place to do so when you entrust it to the people who are closer to the end customer—and in need of the ability to use resources and make decisions to deliver for their stakeholders.

By sharing power and trusting our people to use their time and talent as they best see fit to accomplish goals, leadership satisfies peoples' need for ownership. When a team reaches its achievements, it always feels sweeter when we've been on the playing field actively contributing rather than just standing on the sideline observing. In any facet of life, the need for greater influence over situations, things, and others feels more personally rewarding. Former US Navy Captain Michael Abrashoff understood this reality, stating that "I am absolutely convinced that with good leadership, freedom does not weaken discipline—it strengthens it. Free people have a powerful incentive not to screw up," (*It's Your Ship*, p. 73). The same reason that drives the desire for empowerment and autonomy—to have greater influence over our own lives—also motivates us to ensure that positive outcomes result from our actions.

Motivation via providing a greater sense of ownership and autonomy is an important aspect of empowerment. There are more—and more specific— reasons behind empowerment and trust, however. One such reason is the structure of modern organizations. Flatter group hierarchies in an effort to be more financially efficient and allow for a greater flow of information from the front line to senior management is the trend. This means that organizational structures now demand more decentralization of power to allow staff to react quickly to customer needs, and the organization to adapt to changing business circumstances. Consider the empowerment philosophy at luxury hotel brand Ritz-Carlton, where each employee is allowed to spend up to $2,000 to resolve each guest issue, using their discretion as they see fit, and you will see localized empowerment that actively supports the Ritz-Carlton credo (its purpose).

When we create and communicate purpose to our people, we often don't know the exact steps to make it a reality. We know *what* we want to accomplish but not exactly *how*. For our people, their commitment to the *what* often depends on the degree of their ability to affect the *how*. Again, there's little sense in committing to a purpose we have no control in influencing the fulfillment of. Empowerment and trust allows our team members to help define the paths to success.

> ...a sense of choice means *being able to do what makes sense to you to accomplish the purpose*. It means being able to use your intelligence, take the best course of action, and make effective use of your time.

In short, choice allows you to be performing those activities that you experience as useful. When you are not free to choose, on the other hand, you often find yourself trying to accomplish your work in ways that seem silly or like a waste of time—with resulting frustration. It is impressive how much frustration you can discover in many committed people by asking them about the pointless rules or directives that interfere with their work. (Thomas, *Intrinsic Motivation at Work*, p.54)

Simply allowing choice, providing resources, and demonstrating trust in team members allows them to align their talents more effectively to the purpose. This results in a higher likelihood that they will take a creative, innovative approach to resolve problems. When they have control, people increase their discretionary effort and take initiative to address issues more effectively for customers. They do this knowing that they are trusted to take risks and experiment, occasionally making mistakes along the way, to serve the team's mission. This perspective is also explained and supported by Hiam in *Motivational Management* (p. 141).

Without the ability to use discretion and judgment, none of the experience and learning individuals pick up along the way really matters, and it becomes only about following procedure and the directions of the leader. That leads to a very boring and unfulfilling work experience. As people spend a significant portion of their waking hours on the job, few people stay in such environments for long.

Keeping team members coming back doesn't require a huge degree of talent on the part of leaders; it just requires them to provide others the opportunities to use their own talents more fully. That's it. That's the secret. In doing so, leaders don't give up power—their power just evolves into a more indirect form. The good practices of performance management aren't abandoned either. We still meet regularly with our people, ensure accountability, follow up for progress and coaching opportunities, and ensure that resources are available to achieve our aims. None of that changes.

The great opportunity for leaders lies in the fact that they no longer have to plan both the *what* and the *how* themselves. In freeing themselves from the exhausting work of planning every detail of others' work experience, they also supercharge the motivation of individuals on their teams. As Kouzes and Posner said in *A Leader's Legacy*, "human history tells us something extremely important about human relationships. It tells us that *people want to be free. People want to decide things for themselves. People want to shape their own destiny. People want to be in charge of their own lives.* The most enduring leadership legacies are those of leaders who have set their people free" (p. 49). Deliver that freedom for your people, and you'll also gain a reputation as a leader whose team achieves.

- *What do you do to provide resources and support so your team feels empowered to accomplish their goals?*
- *How do you demonstrate trust and faith in your team members?*
- *Do you provide autonomy to allow your team members discretion in determining how they will reach goals, or do you manage every detail of the work?*

CHALLENGE, PROGRESS, AND ACHIEVEMENT

Like each of the other primary motivation factors discussed, *challenge, progress,* and *achievement* are intrinsic motivators that, with just a bit of planning and follow-up, leaders at every level can tap into. If purpose is the noble cause that points our team members in a general direction, then challenge helps enhance the significance people feel by outlining how hard the journey to our destination will be. Although the road is never fully known, setting a course that engages a good degree of your people's endurance, navigational skills, and other talents will keep them engaged along the way and feeling that the destination is worthwhile when reached. Signposts, mile markers, yardage markers, buoys, project milestones, and many other signs of human endeavor tell us how far we've come, how much of the journey is left, and what effort and resources we still need to reach the destination. Expectations or goals are the destination itself. They provide context to our purpose and operationalize it. Expectations, particularly measurable ones, help the team know when their efforts result in achievement in others' eyes.

Setting individual and team goals to realize purpose is an important motivational tool. Setting expectations clarifies *how* and *how much* teams and individuals positively impact purpose. Doing this allows people to compare their efforts against expectations for impact, and in doing so draw a sense of pride and self-esteem from reaching objectives. Nothing helps validate people's existence at work more than success, and expectations tell us when we have reached it.

No matter how noble we believe the team's purpose is, without expectations it's hard to tap into personal drives to support it. Absent set objectives, people's efforts lack focus, coordination, and proper intensity. Precious talents may also be wasted on activities that don't truly impact purpose. As Lyndia Banks stated in *Motivation in the Workplace*, "it's hard for employees to remain inspired when they have no specific goals. Your organizational and departmental mission statements are good motivational starting points, but to maintain that motivation, you will need to set objectives, or *strategic imperatives*, for your department and your individual employees. Strategic imperatives are limited, specific goals that we can complete and measure" (p. 33).

Setting quantifiable expectations for your people allows them to know how well they are running the race and when it is over. That helps tap into internal drivers by letting staff assess the meaningfulness of the goal and their chances of attaining it. If you've ever tried a triathlon you unlikely started by trying to complete a full Ironman; your effort was more likely aimed at a sprint or Olympic distance race. The reason for this is simple: You assessed your odds of achieving the goal based on your abilities and came up with a choice you felt was most appropriate for you—one that tested your limits but was not unrealistic in your view. Your people do the same in work settings, so the process of setting goals itself initiates this thought process in them that will, ultimately, motivate or demotivate.

Setting expectations is about instilling a sense of achievement in people, and the ability to achieve creates meaning and significance in individuals' work lives. British mountaineer George Herbert Leigh Mallory, in 1924, said he was attempting to climb Mount Everest "because it was there." That is what goals do—they create a proverbial mountain to climb so that we can experience a sense of achievement when we conquer the summit. Time after time, human history has shown us that something deep inside people stirs them to blaze a trail to new accomplishments. Because we need to feel progress and achievement, we commonly create goals when none are given to us. Creating a route on which to use our time and talents just feels better than wandering without direction in the wilderness of our lives.

When leaders set goals for their people, they must ensure that their people are committed too and the leader must follow up on this. When expectations shift before the job is completed and follow-through is lacking, the ability of goals to leverage intrinsic motivation is minimized. "People are energized and more productive when they have memorable priorities to pursue ... If your goals are constantly changing, you can count on constant chaos. Some in your organization will ignore the current goal because experience has taught them that the goal will soon change anyway. Why bother changing course now when another change is probably just around the corner?" (Cottrell, *Monday Morning Motivation*, p. 55)

The second and closely related concept to expectation-setting is *challenge*. When a task lies before us, the level of challenge often affects our motivation to complete it. We quickly dismiss challenges that seem far beyond our capabilities as we don't believe they would satisfy our need for success and achievement. Likewise, we dismiss mundane tasks that are seemingly far beneath us because they aren't a rewarding use of our time and we gain no genuine feeling of achievement from completing them. A worthwhile endeavor that stretches our talents and yet seems achievable best satisfies the drive for challenge. The level of responsibility, influence, impact, challenge, and talent taken to complete the work are all factors we usually consider whether we are looking for the next initiative to complete or the next career opportunity.

The ultimate aim when we set goals and factor in challenge is to conquer them. It's about *achievement*. Setting and achieving appropriately challenging goals enhances self-esteem and validates our existence to ourselves—and in the workplace, to others—making it a strong and universal internal driver. Each of us has likely dreamed of great achievement in some facet of our lives, and over time we calibrate our dreams with our abilities and true level of desire to make them a reality. Distinguishing ourselves is part of the driver for achievement, and that is one of life's little ironies too—we probably spent our youth trying to fit in with the crowd and our adult life trying to stand out from it.

Achievement feels good, and progressing toward it steels our resolve to reach the finish line. The process of leaders working with their people to set challenging but achievable goals that support aligned collective and individual purposes, and provide updates on progress to reach them, are basic but crucial inputs that harness intrinsic motivation. These leadership activities give people worthwhile reasons to apply themselves fully to their work and help your team and the organization be successful. Leaders don't have to have any special talents to complete these tasks. They only need to dedicate proper time and attention to them.

⟶

- *Do you take creating an "appropriate" level of challenge into account in setting goals that motivate your people?*
- *How do you use milestones and progress updates to maintain motivation as people work to achieve goals today?*
- *To support motivation, do you regularly acknowledge your people's progress and achievement?*

⟵

RECOGNITION, APPRECIATION, AND ENCOURAGEMENT

Leadership can indirectly generate motivation that stems from feelings of appreciation, validation, significance, and others having faith in us. When these conditions persist in the workplace, the reward becomes the work environment itself and not what we may receive at the end of a successfully completed job. Recognition that occurs for a job well done and the other plaudits provided to our people, which are external in nature, also help. They are external because although we may recognize and appreciate our own efforts, when others give us these things we feel even more significant to the group. Exactly because our own sense of appreciation is validated against the perception of others we feel our worth is confirmed and our self-esteem is enhanced. Everyone likes being told "you did a great job" or being provided other symbolic acknowledgment of good work.

Others have to give the trophy, plaque, certificate, public recognition, or private thanks for a job done well. Whether individual team members directly receive praise and recognition or see others receive it, along with sincere thanks to the larger group, they see periodic recognition events transform into a culture of appreciation. That then provides a steady flow of motivational energy to our people rather than just a burst now and again. Regardless of its form, this is a universal facet of motivation.

Like the other primary facets of motivation, expressing appreciation, recognition, and belief in others is a low cost means of creating an environment where the drive to perform is enhanced. As leaders, we also directly motivate our team members through our words and actions. This helps to strengthen every relationship and validate others' reasons for remaining in them.

Leaders must also bear in mind the practical business reasons for doing what is right. Harter and Wagner in *12: The Elements of Great Managing* referenced research concluding that employees who don't feel adequately valued are twice as likely to express that they will leave their employer in the next year. They go on to assert that those who rate their organizations highest on recognition and praise in employee engagement surveys are 2.5 times more likely to agree that they are appropriately paid for their work than those who rate their companies lowest (pp. 52-58).

The potential for appreciation to act as a counterbalance to compensation is quite interesting. Have you ever seen or experienced work environments where pressure to perform is high, goals are widely viewed as unrealistic based on prior organizational performance and current resources, and the boss is unappreciative, dictatorial, and generally difficult to work with? Then you may have also witnessed how management has to overcompensate versus market rates in order to attract and retain staff. This drives up operating costs, lowers profit margins, and negatively affects employee engagement and the organization's reputation. Stay bonuses are given out in place of building a more sustainable working culture for people, and monetary compensation is used as a crutch because management's toolbox to attract, engage, and retain people—as well as drive performance—is largely empty. Even though the advantages of using recognition, praise, and belief are numerous and low cost—and the lack of their presence in teams problematic—some leaders find reasons to avoid using them.

> There are several excuses managers and even top executives give for being parsimonious with praise. Some tell their employees up front, "If I don't say anything, you're doing a good job." Other managers dismiss their responsibilities with statements such as "I'm just not very good at giving praise." While they get points for candor, the explanation for defaulting on such a managerial imperative doesn't cut it. Would the same leaders also dismiss themselves from financial results by saying, "I'm not very good with math?" (Harter and Wagner, *12: The Elements of Great Managing*, p. 57)

Rationalizing away the failure to use recognition and praise is no less a dereliction of duty than the failure to be knowledgeable and effective in other areas of operational responsibility. Why would organizations quickly address the latter with leaders, holding them to account, but fail to do so when management undervalues their people? Likely, the answer is that effects are indirect and only observed over time as trends. A manager who lacks operational knowledge is often more quickly revealed than one who fails to lead effectively, unless team performance issues are routinely monitored and held to account. If a team member here or there fails to live up to expectations, management commonly attributes that to having "the wrong people on the bus" rather than having a bus driver who isn't traveling in the right direction. People problems, including lack of appreciation and value, are masked in light of adequate performance and rationalized as "he's hard on his people but the job gets done" if senior managers even come to recognize that people leadership issues exist at all.

If we want to enhance the feeling of value and appreciation in our people, we need to resist the constant pull toward "gap analysis" and "continual improvement" in place of more positive means of performance management. I should be clear here though: *Results matter*. Of course they do. As leaders, we're tasked with obtaining results through others. Some ways of doing that are short-sighted and come at great human costs to organizations and the resources that can build a more sustainable culture of performance, however. Recognition and appreciation are in it for the long game. Leadership with a critical heart isn't sustainable for teams.

We're reminded that paying a compliment that includes the word *but* is often self-defeating. "You did a good job with that customer problem, **but** let's talk about how you could have resolved the issue even more effectively." "You performed well on the latest project overall, **but** let's talk about some opportunities for improvement." When you use the word *but*, no one hears what came before it in your statement. They only commit what came after to memory. In our well-intended efforts to address continual improvement, we fail to drive our people toward performance and keep them in their seats when *but* is a constant part of our vocabulary. After a while, the only thing your people are thinking is, *Whatever I do, it's just never good enough for my boss. Why should I even try? What's the point of even being here?!*

When you begin to pay a compliment and then think about uttering the word *but*, just stop. Put a *period* in place of it in the sentence. Then close your mouth. I bet you'll see a smile on the person you're speaking to. Leave your suggestions for continual improvement to later in the conversation, or leave it for another discussion. Allow some time for your people to digest your compliment and make full use of it to motivate themselves; don't pour cold water on the fire you've just lit in people by recognizing them. Remember, too, that in addition to recognition for performance, the power of appreciating people for who they are is great. When people feel valued not just for what they produce but for who they *are*, a swell of pride and positivity results.

If you want to harness the power of recognition, appreciation, and belief, you have to show it. It isn't enough to think kind thoughts about your people—they can't read minds. They only know how you feel about them when you express your feelings through words and actions. The best leaders in this area actively look for opportunities to recharge their people's emotional batteries by demonstrating that they value and appreciate them, for their work and for who they are as human beings.

We all like to be around people who make us feel good about ourselves, and we tend to work harder for those who validate our presence on the team. "Keep in mind that going above and beyond what is required is a choice, and people are more likely to give when their efforts are appreciated … Extraordinary achievements never bloom in barren and unappreciative settings" (Kouzes and Posner, *A Leader's Legacy*, p.44). Assess how you perform as a leader in this respect. Build appreciation into your leadership processes and, with just a little creativity and humility, you'll find the return on your investment can be great.

- *How do you show appreciation for your people's efforts and personal characteristics today, and not just their accomplishments?*

- *Do you periodically say "thank you" to your people for their achievements and for being part of the team, in both individual and group settings?*
- *Do you use symbolism (trophies, certificates, etc.) and express your appreciation in writing from time to time (using thank you cards, emails, and annual appraisals)?*
- *How do you encourage and express your faith in your team members today?*

INCLUSION AND AFFILIATION

Inclusion is a precursor to empowerment; when individuals are affiliated with the group and participate in activities and decisions that affect them, they're better forearmed with knowledge that allows their talents to be used to good effect. They can make more considered decisions when given the information to do so. In addition, inclusion motivates by tapping into intrinsic drives that people have to feel significant, valued, and respected. Including team members in the narrative of the group and the organization signals this, as well as the willingness to consider their opinions. Better decisions become commonplace in inclusive environments.

As the old (and inaccurate) saying goes, "Knowledge is power." Many leaders hoard knowledge as a precious resource, as if sharing it would decrease their influence and weaken their position somehow. It's much more accurate to say that knowledge, *effectively shared,* is power. Knowledge is only valuable in the hands of people who can act on it to positively affect purpose, otherwise it exists like an unopened book. A palpable feeling of mistrust exists between managers and staff when transparency is lacking. People feel slighted and devalued when information isn't shared, and the message some receive is "You're not important or knowledgeable enough to be trusted with this information. You can't possibly help us with our issue anyways."

Sharing information and including people on the issues facing the team can either be a source of frustration, if withheld, or motivation if provided. As a leader, you get to choose. As Ken Blanchard stated in *The Heart of a Leader*, "when people are given detailed information about the impact of costs and are entrusted to make decisions, their self-esteem rises and customer service improves ... people with information are empowered to make responsible decisions and help the organization succeed" (p. 109). People want to contribute. They want to do good, conquer challenges, feel successful, and be appreciated for their work. They have a better chance of fulfilling these intrinsic motivators if we, as leaders, provide information and demonstrate transparency.

When we include our people on the issues and decisions facing the team, we tap into a considerable pool of talent to bridge the gap between where we are today and future successes. Providing information and inviting them into the discussion is only the start; we've then got to harness the talent sitting at the table through inquiry. Asking questions is another powerful tool, *if* leaders choose to use it regularly. Listening and asking questions are two vastly undervalued skills in staff and leaders alike, and asking questions draws your team members into the conversation. People feel valued and respected when we ask a question because it signals that we value their thoughts and opinions, and will take them into account as we address issues and weigh decisions.

One of the primary benefits of asking questions, listening, and drawing your people into the narrative around performance: They normally come up with solutions, typically creative ones, better ones, or ones leaders hadn't considered. This results because they have a firmer grasp of the context and operational issues they work within and the problems that stand between the organization and the customer. Time after time, if you ask leaders what their people do—then you ask the individual practitioners themselves—two perspectives will result. Sometimes they're quite far apart. As Captain Michael Abrashoff realized in *It's Your Ship*, he may know what's happening on the bridge but below deck is another story. "I began with the idea that there is always a better way to do things, and that, contrary to tradition, the crew's insights might be more profound than even the captain's. Accordingly, we spent several months analyzing every process on the ship. I asked everyone 'Is there a better way to do what you do?' Time after time, the answer was yes, and many of the answers were revelations to me" (p. 15).

Work becomes stimulating when you invite people to think more about it and to share ideas about how to approach problems and reach shared objectives. Team members become driven to come up with innovative solutions when leaders invite them to be a part of the process rather than a passenger in it. Ask good questions—questions that provoke root-cause analysis and invite the weighing up of alternatives—then sit back and listen. Keep the dialogue flowing and encourage debate. You'll find that not only will you implement better solutions, your people will be more committed to seeing them through. They came up with the great ideas, after all.

Remember that the process of inclusion, by definition, draws people further into the center of the group. That's also a good feeling, and one that meets a basic human need for affiliation (think Maslow's hierarchy of needs). We all want to know that we're not alone; that we are part of a tribe where mutual protection and resource sharing are benefits of belonging. We are significant enough to be in the group. That also meets our esteem needs (back to Maslow again...).

If you're to tap into the variety of internal motivators related to inclusion and affiliation, just consider a few issues. The first is whether you often share your opinions and provide solutions to problems at the outset of conversations, or use questioning and listening skills to initially hear what your team members have to say. In addition, team members, individually and in groups, should have regular opportunities to share their issues, problems, and solutions. The team environment should be "safe" so that members feel they can express disagreement and opinions that may differ from the majority. The team environment should also be transparent, with information freely shared, not hoarded.

You'll be happy to know that like other leadership activities to access intrinsic motivators, those related to inclusion and affiliation require relatively simple acts from managers: the self-awareness to understand that you don't have either all the answers, or the best answer in most cases; a focus on inquiry first, where questioning and listening become the primary tools of problem-solving and decisioning; an interest in others' opinions and feelings; and a willingness to let others participate in making and implementing decisions. No rare talents are involved in completing any of these leadership tasks, and they can be learned fairly easily.

- *How transparent is the sharing of issues and information in your team?*
- *Do you use questioning and listening effectively to include people in the process of identifying problems and solutions?*
- *Is your team a "safe" place to share opinions and ideas that may differ from the majority, or yours as a leader?*
- *How often do you implement solutions based on the ideas of your team members versus imposing ones you thought of?*

PERSONAL GROWTH AND LEARNING

The search for knowledge and desire to better ourselves is a natural part of the human experience. Ask many people about their priorities for a future job search, and you'll often hear them express the desire for personal growth. Although this means something different to each individual, the desire to learn new skills, apply knowledge, and become "wiser" is commonplace. In today's workplace, an organization's ability to present opportunities for personal growth and learning isn't just a luxury. It's a necessity if they're to attract and retain quality employees. The priorities of current workforce generations have moved away from job security and steady income toward an emphasis on personal growth and learning, work-life balance, corporate social responsibility, meaningfulness of work, and the ability to apply newfound expertise via career advancement.

To attract, engage, and retain people you have to offer the opportunity for personal growth. This means sitting down and talking to your people about what they want to learn and what opportunities for personal growth excite them. The information you gather will orient you and your available resources toward meaningful learning opportunities for your team members.

Many leaders don't dedicate the same level of planning (or any at all) to learning and development that they do to goal setting and performance management. They assume that, while performing their jobs day to day, team members will just pick up additional meaningful skills and experience. This abandons people to self-development and denies them the benefit of a learning advocate as they seek to grow themselves. When leaders plan for learning and development, including setting goals and deadlines and using a variety of available internal and external resources, the drive for personal growth and learning is much better satisfied. Regular follow-up for progress is important and signals to people that you're willing to help fulfill their need for growth.

If you're still building your skills in personally coaching your people, that's okay. You have to continue to grow those skills, though, because performance management and learning depend on you to apply them effectively as a leader. The good news? If you genuinely, selflessly desire to see others succeed, you can learn how to coach more effectively over time. Just remember that even the most talented people know that practice is critical. The more you use your coaching skills in practice, the more you will hone them. Football (soccer) legend Pelé once said, "Everything is practice." Basketball phenom Michael Jordan once said that you should "practice like you've never won," knowing how important it was to relentlessly pursue excellence. Even with their considerable talents, these sports figures knew that the key to excellence was applying them over and over until they could use them well to gain desired results.

In addition to coaching for skills development that aids people today and personal growth that will help them tomorrow, you can draw upon a number of other resources. Your organization's formal learning and development programs, along with staff who are dedicated to training, are important assets. Review available courses and programs in relation to your team members' desire for learning so you can customize plans for them. Often, the skill required of you isn't a great degree of personal involvement in learning with your people (though this is certainly necessary at times) but the ability to create and follow up on learning plans using the resources around you. Review programs, talk to training staff, and provide courses to help each team member grow in their role.

In addition to formal learning and development programs, use informal mentoring within or outside the team to help your people grow. Based on their learning plan, pair your people with an experienced coworker. You don't have to bear the burden of attending to their performance coaching and personal growth needs alone, and you aren't an expert at everything. Allow your people to learn from others while building their networks within the organization. Even team members who are struggling to perform right now still have a desire to do good work and succeed. We all want to be better versions of ourselves tomorrow than we are today.

Job rotation and cross-training are other means of helping personal growth and skill development, and both involve others in the coaching process. People who expand their skills and abilities contribute to the team in times of shifting workload and priorities, and also enhance their self-esteem and sense of value. In the course of their normal duties, they gain broader knowledge of team issues and the downstream effects of decisions. Another opportunity for personal growth is involvement in project work. Expose team members to different work groups and issues, particularly those that have effects both within and outside the team.

Job enrichment, where your people can take on more end-to-end responsibility for activities in their area, and *job enlargement*, where the scope of the job is widened to include activities not yet familiar, are also means of helping your people grow. Just remember that when you support personal growth and learning for your team, they occur through both successes and failures. Don't make your people run scared at the prospect of committing errors as part of the journey.

> Progress and learning, then, mean expecting and allowing some honest mistakes—and using them as important learning opportunities. If workers are afraid of being punished for honest mistakes, they are likely to play it safe and stay very close to well-established, tried-and-true solutions. Team members will be afraid to trust their judgment and work will become less about doing the tasks in the best possible ways and more about not getting into trouble. (Thomas, *Intrinsic Motivation at Work*, p.165).

The draw of learning and personal growth is strong for those in the workplace. People commonly make decisions about whether they join or remain in organizations based on prospects for personal growth. Work experiences that don't offer this severely detract from meaningfulness and don't fulfill a basic human drive to explore our potential. Use the variety of internal and external resources at your disposal to plan for your people's learning and development, and follow up to ensure it's occurring. While individuals may come on and off your team because you have developed them upward, you will have had more driven and engaged team members who almost certainly performed better as a result. You'll also have grown your own leadership potential along the way.

* *Do you know the learning and development aspirations of each of your people?*
* *Do you make plans for the learning and development of each of your people?*
* *What resources (formal training, job rotation, job enrichment/enlargement, project work, etc.) do you use to help your people learn and grow?*

SOME FINAL WORDS ABOUT MOTIVATION

It's all about relationships. Whether you believe that motivation is a direct process where leaders instill it in their people or they indirectly influence motivation by creating an environment that nurtures it in others, relationships matter. You learn about your people's fears, aspirations, frustrations, desires, talents, motivators, and feelings by building and maintaining relationships with them. Without relationships, leaders are left trying to motivate and manage performance using external means only—carrots and sticks. Transactional approaches to interacting with people and using punishment and reward are outdated, Pavlovian means of managing that fall very short of meeting people's needs in the modern workplace. For the process to be sustainable, they need more than that from you.

John Maxwell quotes Michele Leonard in his book *Encouragement Changes Everything*, who stated that "'life is a great obstacle course, with bends and turns, wins and losses. When you get to the high jump, always remember to throw your heart over the bar—and the rest will follow'" (p. 51). For leaders, this is what motivation is all about—creating an environment that encourages others to throw their heart over the high bar. Once hearts are captured, getting the rest of people to follow along toward the fulfillment of goals becomes a lot easier. Motivation is always about *feelings* and the drive to create meaning for our lives. You can't purchase that with a bonus check.

ACQUIRING TALENT AND BUILDING TEAMS

L eaders either build teams from the ground up or inherit a group, with the latter being far more common. As a "new" leader in the eyes of your group members, you must build a *team*, your team, from the collection of individuals you'll be responsible for. Leaders commonly forget to approach team building in a conscious and purposeful way. This may be due to the sense of urgency to make an impact and ensure that the group continues to function in the face of "battlefield" promotions, or because of other business pressures that tempt supervisors to concentrate just on immediate-term operations productivity. We attempt to skip to the end, assuming our people will adapt well to their new manager because they have to.

It's simply easier to be successful when the team is talented and that talent is deployed in the right places. Success comes more often when we effectively choose our team members. That team seat is precious, and most aren't well suited to occupy it. The second important factor is how, as a new leader of an existing group, you forge an effective, high-performing team by addressing several core issues well.

RECRUITMENT AND SELECTION

One of the most crucial activities you undertake as a leader is talent acquisition. Hiring "right" contributes significantly to building a team that gets results and positively impacts the working culture. We've all witnessed a well-chosen person go on to increase their positive influence on their team and the organization over time. The contrary is also true, as we've all likely observed a coworker, who was a poor fit for the role and work culture, act as a drain on the team's morale and productivity.

The most successful businesses place a high priority on the process of selecting people. They dedicate time, training, and resources to minimizing mis-hires and maximizing the chances of bringing in those who are well-suited for the position, team, and organization. Leaders in these businesses realize that the stakes are high and treat the recruitment and selection process with the seriousness it deserves, because they also understand the implications of managing the process poorly.

THE COSTS OF TURNOVER

When people leave us, we have an empty seat that isn't producing revenue or supporting the seats that do. That empty seat does not help internal or external customers and doesn't move the team closer to meeting its objectives. We have to recruit again, bearing expenses associated with filling the position and onboarding a new team member. The many types of turnover costs emphasize how important talent acquisition is as a leadership function. It isn't a distraction from "the day job" that some leaders may see it as—it *is* "the day job." One of the primary reasons leaders exist? To help the organization ensure that it has the right people to be successful.

The true cost of turnover is nebulous. Many theorists agree, however, that the cost is likely to fall somewhere between the equivalent of six and eighteen months of salary per individual lost for most positions—and could be higher in the case of executives and people with rare skill sets. A number of factors make up the cost. Some are much easier to quantify than others.

The first, and most obvious, cost of turnover is the cost of replacement hiring. There are costs to generate and hire candidates via advertising or other sourcing means. An associated cost, which is harder to pin down, is the cost of time taken up by all those who are involved in the talent acquisition process, including interviewing and selection activities.

The cost of lost productivity is likely the primary expense associated with turnover. While they might save on expense in the short term, empty seats don't make money. We love to see new, smiling faces periodically, but these individuals are unproductive early in their tenure and lower the average productivity of the group—at least temporarily. New hires operate at a fraction of the productivity levels of their experienced counterparts during the first couple of months and may not reach "full" productivity until after six months or more on the job. This may be even longer in the case of newly hired leaders.

Onboarding and training costs are other expense factors. The resources spent to orient staff members and train them to perform their roles competently during the first few months can be substantial. This includes the cost of time, travel, supplies, and lost productivity to the extent that onboarding and training new coworkers takes people away from their "normal" daily duties.

As turnover increases, the cost of replacement hiring may also increase on a per-hire basis. This is because the organization gains a negative reputation, which makes it more difficult to attract the number and quality of candidates needed to fill roles. Roles are left open longer as a result, putting workload strain on the remaining team members. What happens? *Secondary turnover*—where the remaining team members leave due to a perpetual feeling of being short-staffed and overloaded with work.

A lot rides on the recruitment process and the costs of a wrong decision can be very significant, including for your ability to succeed as leader. Managers have periodically told me over the years that they're too busy to engage fully in the recruitment process. Ironically, they are too busy *because* they're short-staffed and need to hire someone. Hiring is something you get to do a lot of if you aren't good at it—because you have to regularly atone for the last hiring mistake you made.

We've only discussed the costs of turnover in determining how substantial wrong hires can impact the team. Imagine if we began including the negative ongoing impact the wrong hires can have upon team morale, productivity, employee relations, company reputation, additional training resources needed to gain basic competence, and their own motivation to achieve. Such thoughts should serve to only increase your awareness of the importance of structured, well-considered hiring.

- *Do you know the turnover rate (voluntary, involuntary, total turnover, turnover within the first year of employment, etc.) within the organization, your business unit, and team?*
- *How has being short-staffed due to turnover affected your team members and your success as a leader?*
- *Does your organization track turnover (involuntary, voluntary, turnover within the first year, etc.) and attempt to estimate its cost?*
- *Do you put off engaging in talent acquisition, including candidate screening, interviews, and providing feedback because you are already "too busy" with work?*

COMMENCING THE RECRUITMENT PROCESS

The first tenet of hiring? *You can't know what you've found until you know what you're looking for.* You have to clearly identify the competencies, skills, experience, and knowledge you're seeking in candidates. Good selection processes naturally stem from this clarity. A common starting point for this is the *job description* for the role. The job description often forms the basis for job advertising and is shared with those involved in the hiring process. It's important to ensure that it properly reflects role responsibilities and the characteristics needed for success.

Hiring managers commonly view the position differently from both job incumbents and the internal/external customers receiving the position's work products. Ask these people about the factors for job success because gaps in your view may lead you to recruit based on an inaccurate understanding of the talents, skills, and experience actually needed. The characteristics you're seeking may also differ from those sought in past due to changing business circumstances. Recruit for the job you have today and tomorrow, not the one you had yesterday. Bossidy and Charan, in *Execution*, comment on this perspective, stating that "the same leaders who exclaim that 'people are our most important asset' usually do not think very hard about choosing the right people for the right jobs. They and their organizations don't have precise ideas about what the jobs require—not only today, but tomorrow—and what kind of people they need to fill those jobs" (p. 109).

You also need to determine what the hiring process will look like. How many interviews will be involved? Who will the interviewers be? What will the interview format look like (one-on-one interviews, panel interviews, assessment days, audio/video interviews)? Will you use any pre-employment assessments? What background check processes will you undertake? You need clarity about the hiring process *before* it commences or you risk it being slow, indecisive, and inconsistently applied to candidates.

Have a sense of realism about your candidate search when you have intake discussions about your team openings. We'd all like to find "the perfect" candidate for the job, but the perfect candidate exists in the theoretical world, not in the real one. We've all likely hired someone for a past role we thought was "ideal" only to watch that person fall off the pedestal we placed them on when we find out that they too have flaws, are human, and aren't the "perfect" match we thought they were.

Some leaders search for months for an ideal candidate without success while refusing to consider other candidates that might lack certain aspects of experience or skills. Often, they do this in the hope that a ready-made new hire will be discovered that "can hit the ground running." Please don't fall into this trap of thinking that being good at unearthing "perfection" allows you to largely ignore onboarding and training activities and throw someone into the deep end of the pool without a life preserver. This is a vain, unrealistic hope.

There's an assumption that experience in one working environment will translate across well to another, but an overreliance on this is a risky recruiting strategy. Don't try to fill an empty seat with a warm body based on experience as a primary driver because the pressure is on. We all know that the result normally ends badly, and if it doesn't it's because you were lucky rather than good at hiring and selection. Don't take that chance as luck isn't a good business strategy.

- *Do you review the job description and main responsibilities of the job prior to recruiting?*
- *Do you have intake conversations with those involved in the hiring process, including HR/Recruiting, so that all are clear about the needed talents and experience of candidates?*
- *Do you clearly define the interview/selection process (how interviews will take place, who will interview, use of background checks and pre-employment assessments, etc.) before it starts?*

GENERATING CANDIDATES

Whether you have the benefit of HR/Recruiting support or have to generate candidates on your own, there are some issues to consider. The first concerns how you position your organization and create job advertising to capture interest. It's common to mistake the job description for a job advertisement. The two are not the same. Sole reliance on what can be a dry outline of the responsibilities and experience needed for the role isn't going to excite many people and undersells what you and your organization have to offer. The goal is to have a truthful and accurate—but also interesting and attractive—explanation about the company and role. A value proposition has to quickly reach the reader if you hope to capture interest from the prospective candidate pool.

Following a description of the role itself, outline the benefits of working with the company, including any additional benefits that might be unique to your business. Include links to company websites and your "careers pages" on social media to allow candidates to research the organization. The quality of information you supply potential hires will quickly leave an impression about the culture and professionalism of your business.

Today's candidate marketplace is overwhelmingly online. Job seekers, including those in more traditional industries such as manufacturing or other labor-based markets, use the internet to source and apply for positions. This doesn't lessen the potential value of other candidate generation streams, but if you are using them in place of an online job advertising presence, you're missing out on the substantial majority of potential candidates. Social media is also an effective means of reaching candidates directly and networking to indirectly source potential applicants. All leaders are talent scouts and should be continually on the lookout for future team members.

Employee referral programs can be a useful tool to generate applicants. By offering an incentive to current employees, usually in the form of cash bonuses, companies can generate additional candidates. The employee has also likely done some basic vetting on their referral to ensure that they would both reflect well on them and be a good, basic fit for the role and organization. Employee referrals may stay longer and be more productive for this reason.

Internships and graduate recruiting are other sources of potential hires, particularly for entry level roles that offer a first step into the job market. These represent the beginning of the conveyor belt in which people are brought into the organization and developed upward into other specialist practitioner or leadership positions. Unlike their more experienced counterparts, graduates come in with very few preconceptions about systems, processes, and resources. There's no debate about "the way we used to do it at Company XYZ" or the fact that the old employer's computer systems were "better" or the breakroom had a nicer coffee machine. The increased ability to mold talent may more than make up for the lack of specific industry experience in certain positions.

The last, but incredibly important, stream of candidates for your role comes from within your own organization. Your internal talent pool holds several potential advantages. Internal candidates come with less inherent risk because the business should already know much more about them than external applicants. You can draw from a behavior and performance record. As the best predictor of future behavior is past behavior, there is simply more information about past behavior that you can assess. The internal candidate is already aware of the organization's working culture, resources, systems, norms, and other information about "the way things are done around here." It's also likely that the candidate has better insight about what they're getting themselves into with an internal position change and can therefore regulate their expectations coming into the position.

As a leader, you won't have to use time and energy familiarizing the internal hire with basic characteristics of the organization, which should allow you to spend more time enculturating them into the team and training them in the role-specific skills to allow them to perform. Their potential time-to-productivity is reduced as a result. Data I gathered for one organization on this subject indicated that not only were internal hires more productive overall on average when compared to their externally hired counterparts, they also remained in the job longer, adding greater stability to the team. In general, the success rate of internal hires can be superior to external hires, and internal hires may also have lower voluntary attrition rates in the crucial first year in the new role. It's during this time when new employee costs, relative to ROI via productivity, are highest.

Promoting staff up internally and replacing them via other internal promotions sets off a chain of job moves that helps organizations increase engagement and productivity and decrease hiring risk and turnover. If an external hire is needed, by hiring at a lower level as a replacement for an internal promotion you're also managing risk. If you're incorrect about your external hire and they aren't successful, the risk of failure in an entry level role will impact the organization less on an individual basis. The pool of external candidates is also greater for such roles.

Wherever your candidates are sourced from, remember that timeliness in processing their applications is important. Qualified candidates commonly have more than one opportunity they're exploring, and businesses that are slow to react to applicant interest risk losing out on good candidates. Applicants are also sensitive to every act their potential employer makes—or fails to make. Slow, complex, and unwieldy processes that are painful for applicants to negotiate indicate a working culture of the same once hired. Manage the impression on candidates via a prompt, decisive, and professional means of guiding them through the hiring process.

- *Do you use a variety of resources to generate candidates for your openings today, including online media, employee referral programs, graduate/internship programs, and internal advertising?*
- *Do you consider your internal talent pool first, or are you in the habit of only looking outside the organization for new hires?*
- *Do you promptly process generated candidates for consideration and know how long it typically takes to fill a job in your organization?*

INTERVIEWING

Having generated candidates, you now need to review applications to narrow the field under consideration. Notice the resume' and cover letter and how they are constructed. What do they tell you about the candidate's organizational skills and thought process? What type of language do they employ—does it demonstrate a bias toward teamwork or a focus on individual achievement? Is the language professional? Are there vague references to achievement, or is there supporting detail? Are the documents concise and focused, or the opposite? Do they have spelling and grammar errors?

Review the job history. Does it demonstrate progression within organizations, or have they built their careers based upon moves from one company to the next? Do they have gaps in employment that need an explanation? Do they have a history of short-term stays in prior positions?

A history of short-term employment in permanent positions indicates a likelihood that the stop on your team may not be for long.

The hiring process is a funnel in which the candidate pool is gradually narrowed based on completing stages within it. Initial candidate selection is more liberal, seeking basic potential matches which indicate that a screening call will be worthwhile. You aren't narrowing down to your couple of "star" candidates at this point; you're determining which candidates are a close enough basic match to warrant getting to know more about them.

Using structured screening and interview questionnaires that are applied to all your candidate conversations is good practice. Without doing so, you have no consistent basis for comparison by which to base your selection decisions. During candidate screening, allow time for the candidate to ask questions also and give them a realistic preview of the job. You want to build excitement for the role but never at the expense of truthfulness about the organization and the challenges of the position. When you build candidate expectations that don't align with reality upon hire, new staff often face disappointment and quickly seek employment elsewhere.

The next stage of the process is typically a personal interview. Often conducted in-person, but also increasingly completed through remote audio/video conversations, you must put in extra preparation to complete personal interviews effectively. There are different formats of personal interviews which you should have already considered as part of your process.

One-on-one interviews are less intimidating for the candidate than interviews involving multiple managers. The one-on-one interview can help put them at ease and perhaps more naturally represent their "true" selves. If you need to conduct more than one such interview to arrive at a hiring decision (it is always good practice to have more than one person involved in the personal interview stage) then additional time will be taken with the candidate, and another visit to the site may be required.

Panel interviews allow for more than one interviewer in the room at a time. The advantage is economizing time, as well as the ability of interviewers to follow up on each other's questions and observe behavior and responses that might not be consistent. The decision-makers are also already in the room at the conclusion of the interview and can discuss their candidate impressions promptly.

Assessment days are the most complex to administer and typically involve more of your HR and management staff. Particularly useful when several identical roles may be hired for at once, this format involves inviting numbers of candidates to the interview at the same time. Interviews are interspersed with group business games/scenarios and pre-employment assessments, where the field may be narrowed down partway through the day. At the conclusion of the day, the interviewers typically get together to hold a robust discussion about the merits of candidate finalists, with a view to quickly making decisions on who to offer positions to.

Prepare for interpersonal interviews to make them more effective. Don't make the mistake of deciding you are either too busy, or such a good judge of candidates that preparation is unnecessary. This is one of the most common mistakes interviewers make. They rush to find the CV, either review it quickly just before or even during the interview, and pay little thought to the questions they'll ask over the course of the discussion. I was once interviewed for an executive role by an interviewer who was fifteen minutes late for the discussion, came without my resume' (and actually asked me for a copy of it during the interview so he could quickly review it), and used foul language during the course of the meeting. Needless to say, I was less than impressed.

Being prepared includes not only reviewing applicant documentation but also coming with a structured interview questionnaire designed to probe for the primary competencies needed for the role. Highlight those questions of particular interest, and take note of any additional concerns you'd like to address based on the application. Make sure you set enough time aside to have the personal discussion, and at a location that offers privacy away from office distractions.

Don't rush through a thirty-minute discussion and determine that you've done a meaningful job of candidate interviewing. Plan to spend closer to sixty minutes or more if you're to thoroughly explore the applicant's suitability. Remember that spending the extra thirty minutes now can save you hours and hours of additional effort trying to unwind a bad mis-hire or coach a much less-than-competent new employee up to the point where they are basically functioning. A small additional investment in time up front may save you and your team considerable pain later.

Greet your candidate, escort them to the interview location, and attempt to put them at ease. Let the candidate know what the interview agenda will be like. Tell them that what they have to say is important, so from time to time you may briefly pause to take notes. Balance your notetaking with personal attention to the candidate, as no one likes to be interviewed by someone who has their nose buried in a notebook instead of looking at them. Will the interview process include a brief tour of the site and/or introductions to coworkers? Make sure everyone is prepared to present professionally.

Use an interview questionnaire that includes questions regarding the primary competencies for the position. This allows you to use the same yardstick to measure candidates against one another and the requirements of the position. This isn't to say that you cannot ask questions that aren't on the questionnaire template, only that the template forms the core of interview questioning content.

Interviewing is a practiced art that taxes our listening and questioning skills. *Behavioral* interviewing questions are commonly used during the interview process. Based on the premise that past behavior predicts future behavior, these questions ask candidates about past work situations in order to understand their behavior during them. Interviewers typically seek information about: 1) the past work situation, 2) the candidate's role in it, and 3) how the situation was resolved or concluded. You may have to ask probing questions in follow-up to gain the information you're seeking. "Tell me about a situation where you were involved in a conflict with a coworker at work," "Provide an example of a time where you dealt with a particularly difficult or angry customer, and how you handled it," and "Tell me about a time that you were given a challenging task or goal and how you approached reaching it" are examples of behavioral interviewing questions.

Competency-based questions involve role plays, scenarios, or other simulation designed to have a candidate demonstrate their competency in a certain area. These can be useful follow-ups to general answers an applicant provides about how they might approach a situation, as such questions ask the candidate to demonstrate it in practice. A mock customer complaint call that a candidate is asked to handle or a skills simulation in which a candidate safely handles a piece of equipment are examples of this.

Probing questions are simply follow-up questions designed to elicit further detail. These questions are the heart of good interviewing, where you don't take an answer at face value and seek additional detail. For example, when a candidate answers "I'm good with people," you may follow up with "What qualities make you a people person?" "Tell me about a time you used your people skills to resolve a customer issue or problem at work," or "Please provide an example of when your people skills helped you overcome objections from a coworker who was initially reluctant to share your point of view." All are probing questions that ask for further detail—evidence of the candidate's assertion that they "are good with people."

Probing questions are intended to help you dig deeper into how a candidate thinks or feels about situations. This might include evidence of what they learned from them, how they took (or failed to take) responsibility for the outcomes, and why they approached situations like they did (i.e., conflict, objections, uncertainty, stress, etc.). This is the fun stuff—getting to know your candidate much better by digging beneath the surface for motivations, values, and behavioral patterns that indicate how they're likely to act in the future. The best interviewers are astute listeners who constantly probe for more information that either confirms or counters their initial impressions.

During interviews, look for contrary evidence. Take note of when you receive an answer that is extreme—for instance, "I always hit the goals I've been given," "I've never had a conflict or disagreement with anyone at work," or "I've never made a serious error in my positions in the past." Later in the discussion, ask a question that seeks contrary evidence ("Tell me about a time that you were given an objective at work and failed to reach it." "Describe a time you had difficulty getting along with one of your teammates."). Individuals who initially stated they always reach their goals inevitably come up with an example of a time they failed to meet expectations when asked again later.

Allow the candidate to do most of the talking. You're conducting the interview to get to know them better through questioning and listening. These two skills are still underrated and vital for leadership. Interviewers who lack good listening and questioning skills and those who fail to prepare well for interview discussions commonly overtalk. Faced with the daunting prospect of "dead air," these interviewers will often "lead the witness" by helping direct candidates toward a desired answer or rationalize away the lack of a response and quickly move on to the next subject. Resist that temptation. Silence allows the candidate to consider their answer, and it places the onus on them to respond. You're likely overtalking if you are doing so more than 20 percent of the time.

Allow time to answer candidate questions and relay information about the position, team, and organization that you feel is important. Such information might include: the expectations and measurables for success in the job; the company's mission and values; the working culture within the team; team structure and composition; and internal career development opportunities. Remember that the company and you as the manager are also being interviewed. As a significant amount of the waking day is spent at work, candidates want to ensure that their time—the one thing they can't manufacture more of—is well spent and that working for you and the organization will be a fulfilling experience.

Expect candidates to come with questions. Questions demonstrate real interest in the position and company, motivation to make a professional impression, and a desire to gain information needed to make a considered decision on a future employer. Candidates hate being asked "What are your strengths and weaknesses?" or "What are your long-term plans for your career?" as these are vague questions that take little thought from an interviewer. Likewise, interviewers themselves disdain "canned" questions from candidates such as "What do you like about working here?" I always hope the candidate will ask a more insightful, targeted question; one that demonstrates they've thought about the information they'd like to glean from the interview discussion, not an off-the-cuff question blurted out because they feel that they must ask *something* as they neglected to prepare.

------------------------------➤

- *Do you prepare for personal interviews by thoroughly reviewing the resume, cover letter, and other information about the candidate?*

- *Do you use structured candidate screening and interview questionnaires to document discussions and compare candidates to one another?*
- *Do you vary your questions (open, behavioral, competency) and use follow-up questioning to dig deeper for the reasons behind a candidate's past behavior?*
- *Do you allow the candidate to do most of the talking while you concentrate on asking good questions and listening intently?*
- *Do you look for contrary evidence and note if your candidate does not come prepared with questions of their own?*

CANDIDATE SELECTION

Those involved in interviews will need to determine whether it's appropriate to advance a candidate to the next step in the process. This includes the progression of applicants to prescreening conversations, from prescreening to personal interviews, through to final interviews, and ultimately to an offer. The risk of rejecting qualified candidates is just as great as advancing unsuitable candidates.

There's danger as candidate numbers increase. A temptation to scan for buzzwords and desired experience may exist, quickly rejecting the rest. As a result, the pool might be rid of wholly unsuitable candidates but may also be deprived of hidden gems where aspects of talent and skill are overlooked. It helps immeasurably if you define the required and desirable traits, skills, and experience prior to the review process, knowing of course that talents are the hardest to uncover on paper.

If in doubt, sort toward inclusion unless you have numbers of highly matched applicants already. It's crucial to put skills and experience in proper perspective for each position, understanding that they're only part of the characteristics for success. An individual is more than just the sum of their skills and experience. Talents and competencies should also be important factors in candidate consideration.

Where the process advances to personal interviews, keep some selection considerations in mind. First, use a structured interview process by which the core competencies for the job are explored. Those involved in interviewing should also understand the process, the tools used (questionnaires, pre-employment assessments, background checks, etc.), and the selection criteria.

Candidate assessments should be structured. This might include Likert rating scales for core competencies, a ratings matrix that weights the relative importance of each primary selection criteria (i.e., talents, skills, experience listed individually) along with a rating for each to come up with some overall score, stack ranking by interviewers for comparison, or some other method. This reduces the reliance on intuition, "gut feel," and snap judgments to come to a more considered decision.

At each hiring stage, it's good practice to have a brief, interactive discussion between all interviewers after the end of interview discussions. This allows interviewers to explain their views about a candidate and challenge each other in order to come to well-considered decisions. There are no more important decisions that leaders make than those regarding people. Best practice at work is formed through active discussion and debate so that the pool of knowledge is wide. Hiring is no different and is a crucial leadership responsibility that shouldn't be short-changed via a lack of direct interaction between decision-makers. The implications of rushing to unwise judgment are significant:

The old maxim says "You marry as is. You get any change if you're lucky." The same is undoubtedly true of hiring. Obviously, this doesn't mean that you can't help a person to learn and grow. It simply means that when you hire someone, you are hiring a human being blessed with certain predictable patterns of emotion, learning, memory, and behavior. If these patterns are not to your liking, you are going to have to expend tremendous effort to eradicate them and forge entirely new ones. Since this effort would be more usefully deployed elsewhere, it will serve you well to take extreme care when inviting a new person onto your team. (Marcus Buckingham, *The One Thing You Need to Know*, pp. 73-74)

Skills are more easily taught—but an individual's talents, competencies, thought processes, principles, and values evolve over the long term, if ever. During the interview, an overemphasis on skills and experience may come at the expense of enduring patterns of thought and action that likely impact performance much more.

The lack of timely candidate feedback slows down the hiring process, increasing expenses associated with having the "empty seat" and risks losing qualified candidates to competitors who move more quickly through the hiring process. Speed is not an adequate alternative to a thorough and structured selection process, but organizations have to work both well and quickly in recruiting. Delays signal an indecisive and disorganized approach to candidates, who begin to rethink how attractive the job and company really are.

Interviewer feedback also needs to be meaningfully detailed. Supervisors commonly state that a candidate "just isn't a fit." Stating the candidate was "great" is of no use either. Such feedback doesn't help others understand the rationale in selecting or rejecting a candidate, or help to target future candidates for a better match. When faced with a legal challenge, if you use no structured process, take no notes, and give "not a fit" feedback you put your organization at greater legal risk—in addition to neglecting your responsibility to effectively hire. You should be able to articulate specific reasons that led you to accept or reject a candidate. If you can't then you are either using the poor practice of "gut feel" or need to think further through the rationale behind your decision.

Pre-employment assessments are also commonly used to aid in candidate selection. These assessments provide additional information that might shed light on a candidate's match for the role, organization, and working culture. They may confirm your impressions or might contain information of concern to follow up on. Assessments should be applied to all candidates when your organization reaches the appropriate stage in hiring. Pre-employment assessments are a tool and not a panacea for an organization's candidate selection ills. They should also never be used as a sole determiner in selecting or rejecting candidates.

As the hiring process moves toward conclusion and finalists are chosen, background checks can be useful. Education, employment, criminal record and other background information may be checked in compliance with relevant employment law. These checks can validate the accuracy and truthfulness of information a candidate has provided during the hiring process. Former supervisors and coworkers can discuss their experience of working with the candidate and their perspective on the applicant's suitability for the job they are interviewing for.

---------->

- *Do you have interactive discussions with other interviewers to determine a candidate's suitability?*
- *Do you consistently use the candidate interview questionnaires, background checking, and pre-employment assessment tools that may be available to you?*

- *Do you provide specific and detailed feedback regarding why you recommend or reject candidates?*
- *Do you emphasize interviewing only for skills and experience, or do you also look for competencies and talents that you can adapt and mold to the job?*

← ▬▬▬▬▬▬▬▬▬▬▬▬▬▬▬▬

OTHER HIRING CONSIDERATIONS

All of us bring our own particular mix of experiences, perspectives, principles, values, and thoughts into the hiring process. We each view the world through a unique lens that is colored by these factors. We live in certain areas, hold particular jobs, engage in various hobbies, pursue specific studies, and attend one school or another that is "good" depending on the preconceptions we've formed over a lifetime of experiences and influences. In a word, we all can hold *biases*. As people decisions are the most important ones we can make, it's important to acknowledge the existence of our own personal biases. We can then guard against their influence in hiring decisions as they can detract from the integrity of the selection process.

The first bias is *stereotyping*, where we attribute certain characteristics to all members of a particular classification of people rather than treat each person as an individual. For a very long time, this has caused discrimination based on race, gender, age, ethnicity, and other characteristics. Such tendencies not only detract from the quality of your hiring decisions but are also socially irresponsible and may even contravene employment laws. "All persons who were a captain of a sports team must be good leader" or "All accountants and IT staff are introverts" are examples of stereotyping.

Halo and Horn Effects refer to situations where a single characteristic about, or answer from, a candidate is either very attractive (Halo) or very "bad" (Horn). Those involved in hiring make an interview decision solely on the basis of that one aspect without considering the rest of the information gathered about the candidate. This is the ultimate example of extremism in selection decisions. Such responses almost certainly should not have been a sole determiner and may not even be directly relevant to the ability to do the job. For example: "She had this bad habit of tapping her fingers while thinking of an answer to my questions," "He said that what he enjoyed most about his last job was working in an environment with open idea-sharing. Senior management doesn't do a lot of that here. He won't like it at all," or "She graduated from ABC University. She's going to be smart enough to do this job then."

Comparison error is another form of bias, where rather than being judged on individual merits, candidates are compared with current or past team members and judged favorably or unfavorably on that basis—i.e., "His appearance and manner reminds me a lot of John, who was a high-maintenance employee who was hard to manage. I don't want another problem on my team," or "Her enthusiasm reminds me of Luisa, who is enjoyable to work with and is supportive to the team. She ought to do well in the job." In addition, we are positively biased toward others whose appearance, manner, background, or other characteristics closely resemble our own. While our minds and heart might favor diversity, subconsciously we work against this desire.

Validity-related biases are any other biases we hold that act as determiners of a candidate's fate that are unrelated to their ability to perform the role. Examples of such bias include: "He's not a golfer. He's not going to be able to relate well and build relationships with our other senior managers on that basis," "She has children, and I bet that will be a problem in terms of her ability to work the schedule we require," or "I've never heard of the university she graduated from. Her educational background isn't a match for us."

The processing of internal candidates is another issue to explore. We've touched on the potential advantages of hiring internally, but the best candidate for the position, wherever found, ought to be considered for hire. You should also consider the need to balance continuity on teams with the benefits of bringing in new ideas and perspectives from outside the organization.

There are issues regarding internal candidates to consider. The first is how processing internal applications should be the same. When internal candidates are treated substantially different than their external counterparts, hiring integrity is risked. Overconfidence that "we know" internal candidates leads to complacency where interviews are just casual conversations. Assumptions about job suitability may be based on our relationship with the employee, or with the supervisor that currently manages them, rather than their ability to perform the role.

> Many jobs are filled with the wrong people because the leaders who promote them are comfortable with them. It's natural for executives to develop a sense of loyalty to those they've worked with over time, particularly if they've come to trust their judgments. But it's a serious problem when the loyalty is based on the wrong factors. For example, the leader may be comfortable with a person because that person thinks like him and doesn't challenge him, or has developed the skill of insulating the boss from conflict. Or the leader may favor people who are part of the same social network, built up over years in the organization. (Bossidy and Charan, *Execution*, p. 116)

The process for considering internal candidates should be no less rigorous than that for external applicants, and the same selection process should be applied. When interviewing is consistent, there's a better chance that the most qualified applicant will be hired (therefore potentially contributing more to team success and making their new boss look good!). Avoid the mistake of hiring candidates based on the "comfort factor" rather than the one best-placed to perform the role.

Consider a couple of differences in processing internal candidates. The first is responsiveness to applications. The internal recruitment process, if poorly administrated, can cause relationship problems between employees and the organization that can hasten their move toward the door. Internal candidates are, at the very least, owed prompt acknowledgement of their application and the courtesy of an initial screening conversation. Even if it's widely held that the internal candidate is unlikely to be qualified for the position, the conversation helps the business better understand the employee's motivations for applying, their career development aims, and their talent, skills, and experience. Common courtesy also signals to the employee that the company is serious about career development and internal hiring.

As another basic show of respect, you should provide internal applicants timely feedback about the outcome of their application directly via conversation and not email. Provide an internal candidate as much frank feedback as is appropriate, along with advice for addressing areas for growth, in order to place them in a better position to be considered for roles in the future.

Unlike external applicants, information such as annual appraisals, commendations or other formal recognition, and records of performance and behavior issues are accessible. In addition, you can speak to the employee's current and former supervisors and other stakeholders or recipients of the employee's work products. There may also be additional historic data on employee performance to consider. You have more information available to understand the internal applicant's qualifications for the position and decrease the risk of a mis-hire. It would be unwise not to use it.

- *Do you use all the information at your disposal regarding internal candidates to ensure they are a good match for the position and team?*
- *Do you use the same thorough interview and selection approach with internal candidates that you do with external applicants?*
- *Do you ensure that prompt and personal feedback on the progress and outcome of applications is provided to internal candidates?*

A WORD ON THE OFFER PROCESS
AND PREHIRE CONTACT

Once you've chosen a candidate of interest, you need to "close the deal" and get them to say yes to your employment offer. It's common to have a follow-up call with them after the final interview but before you make the offer call. The intent is to gauge the candidate's interest in the position and company, address any questions or concerns they may have, and understand what their financial and other requirements are in order to join the team. Forearm yourself with as much information as possible in order to understand whether you can meet their employment requirements and ensure the match is a good one. This helps ensure a greater likelihood of a "yes" answer when you do make the offer call itself.

Prepare for the offer call (create a checklist of the items you will cover). Have all the relevant steps in the hiring process been completed? What subjects will be covered in the call (i.e., compensation structure and details, benefits, start date, onboarding and training plan outline, requirement for background checks, etc.)? Do you have the needed information on each of these subjects? In addition, having an HR representative on the offer call itself may be wise, as it allows a professional to address the more detailed questions about compensation and benefits so the candidate has the information they need to promptly consider the offer.

TEAM BUILDING

Rather than build a team from the ground up, we typically inherit an existing group when we take on a new leadership role. How that group operates as a team—and evolves its efforts and results under your leadership—is a core function of your role. Team effectiveness depends overwhelmingly on the relationships you build and maintain with your people, as well as those between team members themselves. Your approach to your interactions based upon the unique characteristics, motivations, and goals of each person will be a crucial determiner of your success in getting results. Intercede too much and you damage trust and relationships and underutilize the human capital at your disposal. Be too laissez faire, and you abandon your people to circumstance and cede control over their outcomes. The ability to synergize efforts for mutual benefit is a core talent of leading. Indeed, that's why the role exists.

Team building is often discussed as if it's an easy process—follow the recipe, and "Wow!" you have a high performing, happy work team. In reality, it takes substantial time, effort, and focus from you. It doesn't happen quickly, and it requires continual attention to maintain what has been built. You also need to attend to it promptly. In the early days of your leadership, your new group of individuals has a heightened sensitivity to all that you say and do. Their opinions of your general competence and ability to make a positive difference in their work lives will all form quickly. It will be measured in days and weeks. It's much harder to change an opinion once it's set, so first impressions matter greatly for you as the new leader.

You'll be tempted to make changes to "make your mark" and hasten the forging of a new group identity. Tread carefully here, as it's not uncommon for leaders to come in with preconceptions about the team's performance or problems by reviewing the numbers. You may also make snap judgments based on brief interactions you've have had with your inherited team members. If you rush to imprint your leadership on the group, you may force change before relationships with individuals are formed and the context of team activities understood.

Watkins, in *The First 90 Days* (p. 168) analogized building a team with repairing a leaky ship in midocean. You have to attend to the repairs, but not so quickly and drastically that the ship doesn't make it to port. Ask even more questions and listen at the beginning of your tenure so that you'll gain a better overview of how the group and its performance came to be. The reliance on rushed and radical change to make a leader's mark sometimes stems from ego rather than a sense of serving the greater good.

The rushed, knee-jerk decision to change the way the group operates (and possibly even the players themselves) with little forethought sends a message to the group about the type of leader you will be. That picture won't be very flattering. You've not taken the courtesy to get to know your people and understand their ideas and opinions, and you've left them out of the decision-making process around these quick changes. Team members are left with the impression that ego and ignorance will guide your approach to change management. Another trap to avoid is not thinking consciously about the team-building process at all, believing that it will just organically occur without investing time and attention to your people up front:

> Many new as well as experienced managers do a lousy job of meeting, much less getting to know their associates. Nothing is more important (after understanding your mission) than providing quality time to your associates in both group and one-on-one settings. Your willingness to meet with your team and invest your time in listening to their ideas, issues and concerns is an important tool for building your leadership credibility. The perception that 'you care' is powerful and priceless. Establishing and maintaining an effective communications program is core to a leader's role. In the first few days and weeks of a new leader's tenure, the communication should be more about getting to know each other than about formal operations reports. (Petro and Petty, *Practical Lessons in Leadership*, p. 80)

BUILDING TEAM IDENTITY–
RITUALS, SYMBOLS, CELEBRATIONS

Constructing team identity is the first step in team building. It is so obvious that it's sometimes overlooked, but to start, everyone needs to understand who is a part of the team and who isn't. Once the members understand who their coworkers are within the team, how the team structure looks, and who their direct supervisor is, they can begin building relationships with new members and will redefine relationships with existing members based on changes in formal positions and informal roles. Team membership status adds another layer of pressure to "do our part" as our behavior and productivity affects others in the group. Membership signals interdependence, particularly in teams with specialist roles.

Implementing symbols, rituals, and traditions also helps build team identity. Whether it's the Friday "casual day" or team lunch, the group meeting scheduled every Monday morning, or your biweekly one-on-one meeting with each team member—all are indicative of team identity. If you're in the group, then you can expect to be a part of these regular activities that are unlikely to happen in the exact same way at the exact same time elsewhere.

Recognition, celebration, and engagement activities are also important to team building. How the team celebrates birthdays, anniversaries, or other special events associated with team members sets it apart. For example, in one organization it became tradition for me to buy a cake for each team member's birthday or anniversary. I'd regularly come back with some humorous cartoon cake that was in stock at the local supermarket, personalized with the team member's name. It was a small gesture but became our team's "thing." In another organization, it was tradition for one of the staff members to sing "Happy Birthday" loudly and off-key to other employees. She had a wry sense of humor and loved the responsibility of singing, and the staff seemed to love it too. Traveling trophies, peer recognition, and other ways of celebrating and appreciating one another also become ingrained in the fabric of team culture.

If you're going to make being on the team a unique experience for your people, and one that is likely witnessed by others in the business, then make it something special. Get people outside your team enviously asking, "Why doesn't my team do something great like that?!" If you think about elite teams, the members proudly identify themselves with the group. Membership itself is highly valued, and individuals know that the price of entry and continued membership is living up to the high standards set within the group. A positive identity signals to all that entry onto your team means that their status is enhanced by association, but along with the prestige comes obligation. That esprit de corps becomes a source of pride for team members that propels the team toward consistent effectiveness, and from success to success.

- *Are members clear about who is on the team and the roles each member plays?*
- *Do you have established rituals that are known on your team and differentiate it from others?*
- *Do your team members understand how others are dependent upon them to perform well in order to accomplish their own work?*

SHARED PURPOSE AND MEANING

Teams are more than just collectives of people who understand that they are "in the group." The group doesn't just exist to celebrate birthdays and anniversaries or hold meetings to socialize and share a general sense of appreciation. Effective teams have both shared purpose and meaning.

Purpose is the compass needle of performance effort; it points the way to the intended destination and instills drive to make the journey successful. Purpose answers the question of "Why am I on the team?" This is the benefit of context, without which an environment that effectively supports productivity isn't possible. Lacking direction, apathetic team members allow inertia to rule as they become passengers on the journey rather than pathfinders. There's little point in putting forth a full and conscientious effort if no one understands to what end it will come.

Katzenback and Smith assert that "the best teams invest a tremendous amount of time and effort exploring, shaping, and agreeing on a purpose that belongs to them both collectively and individually" (from the article "The Discipline of Teams" in the Harvard Business Review book *Building Better Teams*, p. 28). This may be the case in some instances, but typically a team's purpose is largely set prior to members joining. In addition, individuals come and go as teams evolve. These new team members don't mutually explore and agree on purpose prior to joining the team; instead they decide that the team's purpose, as known to them at the time, is appealing enough to interest them.

What happens on effective teams? Individuals witness the environment in which they operate evolve, and as a result the purpose of the team may need to be recast in light of changing circumstances. Team members then have the opportunity to shape purpose in order to respond effectively to the new reality. The insightful leader uses changing circumstances to allow others to have a voice and leverages the expertise of their people to prepare the team for success as they head off down a different path.

Often, the new leader treats his or her arrival as just such an opportunity to review purpose and listen to team members' input. Reviewing and potentially updating the team's mission and vision, if they exist—or creating them if they do not—is an important step in setting direction. As Marcus Buckingham stated in *The One Thing You Need to Know*, "you, the leader, must be clear about whom you are choosing to serve because we, your followers, require it of you. If we are going to follow you into the future, we need to know precisely whom we are trying to please … Tell us explicitly, vividly who our main audience is. Tell us whom we should empathize with most closely. Tell us who will be judging our success" (pp. 150-151).

Paint a picture of what successful outcomes look like. The point, after all, isn't just to serve but to serve well and meet both the customer's expectations and the company's objectives. That picture needs to be clear and vivid in team members' minds. They will then know why the team exists, who they serve, and what success looks like.

These efforts alone aren't enough to build a resilient and effective team. Leadership also needs to create individual and collective meaning. There's a difference between *purpose* and *meaning*. Purpose is the direction and reason for the team's operation. It rationally bounds efforts to serve particular audiences. An example of a statement of team purpose: "The team's mission is to grow the portfolio of loans at competitive margins by ethically helping customers with their borrowing needs. In doing so the team helps the organization to reach Return on Equity, Return on Average Assets, and Loan Portfolio Size objectives."

This might be an appropriate mission statement for a loan production team at a bank, but it likely does little to inspire individuals to give their all to the cause. It also doesn't respond to the emotionally-based need for meaning, significance, and personal motivation. The mission statement described above benefits the organization and its customers, but nothing is mentioned about the employees.

No one becomes excited only at the prospect of bringing commercial success to their masters, or frankly, even with the thought of merely putting a smile on a customer's face. A deeper reason must exist for why we spend the majority of our waking hours away from our loved ones, fighting traffic at the beginning and end of the workday. How do we make a worthwhile contribution to bettering our own lives, those of others, or leaving the world a better place? These are fundamental questions that we ask ourselves at some point in our careers when achieving key performance indicators (KPIs) and earning that 3 percent raise and bonus seem increasingly hollow. We wonder, *What else am I here for?*

The insightful leader helps answer this question. Whether it's making loans at the bank, moving freight in the warehouse, or attending to customers in the shop or call center, leaders who help their people find deeper meaning in their work unleash greater engagement, effort, and productivity from them. When we know that our contribution runs beyond the company's "bottom line" and customer satisfaction metrics, we associate our positions with contributing to the greater good.

Tell your people about the impact of their work on the quality of life of their customers and the communities in which they serve. Explain how their work allows the organization to make and fulfill corporate social responsibility commitments. Share heartfelt stories about those who've been impacted for the better. If you can weave a narrative of how work efforts result in improvements to the state of humanity, even if it's one person at a time, you'll create meaning that keeps people enthusiastically fighting the crowd each day to get into work and make more good happen.

- *Does your team have a shared purpose that is written and known to all team members?*

- *Do your people understand who they serve (the end customer for their efforts) and what success looks like?*
- *Do you help team members find meaning to work by sharing stories of their positive impact, beyond helping the organization's "bottom line"?*

TALENT IDENTIFICATION AND GAP ANALYSIS

The master skill of team building is, unsurprisingly, the same skill that's so imperative to success in other leadership competencies. It's about getting to know your people. To build a successful team, you need to know who deserves to be part of it and which roles members should play to help the team achieve. This isn't a surface attempt to learn a bit about your people; you have to engage fully, investing you time, energy, and attention on your people at the group and individual levels to understand dynamics among team members. "Talent masters do not resort to vague clichés or rely on batteries of mechanistic tests to assess talent. Instead they study the behavior, actions, and decisions of individuals, and link these to actual business performance. Their observations are rigorous, specific, and nuanced … In a word, they work to become *intimate* with their talent—that is, to know the essence of each individual" (Charan and Conaty, *The Talent Masters*, p. 8).

A key leadership success factor for you? Understanding where individual talents lie, their ability to be applied for individual and group success, and how they can be sustained and grown over time. If excellence is where talent and passion collide, then you must understand where both lie within individuals if you're to build a team that achieves. Obviously, you can't leverage talents if you don't know what they are. Once you know this, you can consider how to position them to be maximized for goal attainment.

The most obvious example of talent identification and positioning is in team sports. There's a reason Michael Jordan and Kobe Bryant never played center in professional basketball, or why Pelé, Diego Maradona, Lionel Messi, and Cristiano Ronaldo didn't forge careers as goalkeeper in football (soccer). In rugby, Jonah Lomu played the wing for New Zealand and Jonny Wilkinson was a fly-half for England—for specific reasons. On any consistently great team, you'll find a coach who is adept at finding where player talents lie and then positions them to capitalize on those talents for team success.

There's a natural human bias toward negativity. It's built on the premises of continual improvement and risk management, and other methodologies designed to focus on management by exception. This has become ingrained in business, where the default is often working on weaknesses rather than playing to strengths. When this happens, real consequences for staff morale and engagement manifest themselves. When we do nine things "right," two of which are exceptional outcomes, and one thing "wrong," where does the focus of the boss' conversations with us typically lie? On the unacceptable deviation from the norm.

When you fail to acknowledge talents and accomplishments in favor of concentrating on weaknesses, you signal to your staff that you'll view nothing they do as good enough. They come to believe that they're playing a game they can't win. When that happens, you see decreasing engagement and effort while people update their resume to find a place they can feel a greater sense of self-worth and accomplishment.

There's a reason no (sane) coach would ever play Cristiano Ronaldo in defense or tell Tom Brady he should work on his kicking game in American football. In all fairness to both, these might be relative weaknesses, but they're also skills these players are unlikely to ever use. Instead, the coach simply places these great athletes in a position to leverage their strengths. There's a saying about the dilution of talent by concentrating on too many things: "Jack of all trades, master of none." While team members all have areas of opportunity for improvement that can be made known to them as a part of personal growth, the effective leader put these "weaknesses" in proper perspective. In doing so, they help their teams accomplish more, and more often.

In addition to identifying, positioning, and properly focusing on talent, leaders who build effective teams also unearth the *passions* of their people. An obvious link exists between motivation and performance, and when we have passion—a strong and enduring interest that we feel emotionally connected to—we're strongly driven by opportunities to pursue passionate purpose. Passion not only collides with talent but also motivates us to use it more fully. It does so because talent now dedicates itself to the very strong and enduring interest that moves our hearts and minds.

Just like talent, leaders can't unearth the passions of individuals without engaging with them. Ask your people directly. Observe the issues they tend to speak about and act on promptly with conviction and energy. Find out what drives them in times of adversity and what social and community-based pursuits they enjoy. Identifying talent is only half the job; learn what pursuits team members want to apply their talent to most. You will supercharge their potential for achievement if you place them in a position to do so. People will achieve to the degree they can employ their talents, particularly when those talents are focused upon passionate purpose.

- *How well do you know your people's strengths and areas for growth?*
- *Do you let team members leverage their strengths in their roles, or just concentrate on improving areas of weakness?*

- *Do you know what each of your people are passionate about, and are you harnessing that passion for their benefit and the team's?*

←————————————————————————

THE RULES OF ENGAGEMENT AND
SHARED STANDARDS OF BEHAVIOR

The most successful teams have rules regarding behavior, decisioning, collaboration, conflict management, and how members should represent themselves and the group. It becomes a source of pride when "the way we do things around here" is a virtue and represents excellence. Norms can either be overtly codified or permeate your team culture implicitly. In either case, norms bring further meaning to team membership and the obligations that go with it.

The most obvious examples exist in the military and sporting realms. Elite military units have high and uncompromising norms, as operational excellence is literally a matter of life and death. For those in the United States Navy Seals, France's GIGN, the United Kingdom's Special Air Service (SAS), and other military special forces, being in the group is deeply meaningful and a source of pride because the price of entry and continued membership is very steep.

In sports, the difference between a single championship and a dynasty is the norms that support consistent achievement. Ask those involved with hockey's Edmonton Oilers in the 1980s; American football's New England Patriots over the last twenty years; basketball's LA Lakers, Boston Celtics, and Chicago Bulls since the 1980s; football's Real Madrid, Manchester United, Juventus, and Bayern Munich; or Cricket's West Indies and Australia national teams. Individuals on those teams will tell you there was a "way we do things around here" at the time, driven by leaders and upheld by team members, that built and maintained their dynasties.

Norms help build and maintain mutual accountability, which is crucial to team success. It's common to build norms concerning teamwork and collaboration. Individuals need to understand that, despite differences in the quality of their relationships with others, the expectation is to work constructively with all team members. Effort, information, or talents important to team success shouldn't be withheld because of personality differences that make working alongside some people more fulfilling than others.

Set out the norms for conflict handling and resolution too. This may include reinforcing that conflict is a part of work and life, it is inevitable, and when it occurs it's to be handled with a view toward problem resolution and moving on without harboring ill-feeling. Conflicts arise, we resolve them, and we put them behind us. Norms around conflict management help bring issues to the surface early and allow parties to discuss them openly. Very similar norms may be applied to complaint-handling, including the fact that discussing complaints openly with coworkers not involved in the issue or out in the open in customer-contact areas isn't appropriate. Set the norms around how, where, and when complaints and conflict are to be addressed.

Consider too how your team shares information, opinions, and ideas and how issues are addressed and decisions are made. It isn't about the outcomes themselves; it's about how you arrive at them. Setting norms around problem resolution can influence effectiveness in handling them. You should also determine how your team shares information. Is it ad hoc and informal, with a free-flow of information between all team members? Do team members vet it first then share it, but in some cadence of group meetings where members freely speak at that time? Do you encourage members to discuss problems early and openly, or do they use another method?

When we determine when, how, or whether performance or behavior issues are addressed, these become norms. It's clear that the norms set become aspects of team culture; a culture that either contributes to or detracts from goal attainment and team members' experiences. They also, crucially, affect your success as leader as judged by team results.

- *What norms for behavior (teamworking, collaboration, complaint-handling, information sharing, decision-making, accountability, etc.) exist on your team?*
- *How are people familiarized with your team's norms, including new team members?*
- *Do you currently have "advertised" norms for behavior that you are not upholding as a leader by enforcing consequences?*

TEAM STRUCTURE

Ensure that your team has the supporting resources and structure to accomplish the aims that you've set for it. Shape the environment for your people. Pave the road and cut down the fallen trees that block it. Equip the team with GPS, tools, and the right vehicles for the journey. Give them the means to call for help when problems arise, set up mile markers to help them assess progress, and alert them when they are off course.

In addition to reviewing systems, processes, and structure, explore the activities your people undertake today and how they prioritize them, why they think these tasks are crucial, and how they connect to strategy. This is very important, particularly during changes in purpose that leaders implement during team building. Understanding team members' thought processes as they carry out their work also tells you about their understanding of purpose and how they undertake work in relation to it.

Team structure considers the roles people play, hierarchy, subgroups that regularly collaborate, geography versus business line, and the appropriateness of "matrix management." Structural resources include policies and procedures, workflows, systems, and automation. Strike a balance between freedom and formality. Every task doesn't require a written procedure and ten-step process. There does need to be enough structure to focus efforts properly, maintain consistency of outcomes, and minimize repeated or large errors. Structures should *always* enhance the odds of the team reaching expectations for performance.

Successful execution is based on clarity, and clarity is based on simplicity. To accomplish your aims, make structures as straightforward as possible. Complexity causes people to disengage and work to their own devices, which is the exact opposite of what you want when you're seeking predictable, high-quality work. If you've ever cast aside the twenty-page manual found in the flat-pack furniture you're trying to put together in favor of putting that set of drawers together yourself, you know what I mean.

As structure helps breed clarity, implement it for key tasks. For the sake of decentralized decision-making, it's common to neglect implementing enough meaningful structure. Well-constructed frameworks needn't inhibit local decision-making. There can still be process and structure that allows for autonomy to make local decisions to positively impact the customer.

Analyze workflows and processes to see if they require re-engineering to better support the team in the future. Ensure that policies and procedures are still relevant, or otherwise update or discard them. When required, create new policies and procedures to provide proper guidance. Consider the virtue of simplicity whether you're creating these from scratch or just updating them. Where documented policies, procedures, and workflows exist—simple and with visual guides—new and experienced staff will possess a useful reference tool.

Setting expectations and using KPIs to support performance is another aspect of putting structure in place. Katzenbach and Smith, in their article "The Discipline of Teams" in the Harvard Business Review Press book *Building Better Teams* acknowledge the importance of expectation setting. They state that "the best teams also translate their common purpose into specific performance goals … if a team fails to develop specific performance goals or if those goals do not relate directly to the team's overall purpose, team members become confused, pull apart, and revert to mediocre performance" (p. 29).

Documenting personal goals increases the chances that they are attained. The same premise holds true on business teams. Purpose provides a compelling reason for our continued team involvement. Appropriately created and fulfilled goals realize purpose through achievement. Clear evidence points to the relationship between clarity of expectations and increased performance, which helps fulfill purpose. KPIs also help your people understand how you'll assess progress and success and assist them in auditing their own performance.

The final main consideration is resources. The perceived lack of resources to bridge purpose, performance expectations, and operational results can be a major frustration that disengages staff and causes lower morale and increased turnover. There's nothing more frustrating than having responsibility without authority and goals without the means to achieve them. Failure to address this situation is one of the enemies of successful team building and a primary reason team members seek career opportunities elsewhere.

- *Do you periodically review structure, systems, processes/ procedures, workflows, and resources to see whether they still effectively support the team's goal achievement?*
- *Do you know how your people feel today about the resources provided to them to do their work successfully?*
- *Do KPIs and expectations exist on your team and are they well known to your people?*

Section 4

MANAGING PERFORMANCE

This is where "the rubber meets the road" for managers. Great ideas come cheap. We all have a million of them. The trick is to translate them into action, and there's no substitute for purposeful action when it comes to winning in business. Performance management is the bridge between ambitious strategy and successful execution. It's the core reason leaders exist—to obtain successful results through others' work. When you consistently accomplish that, you multiply your impact exponentially and your value to the team and organization skyrockets.

ACCOUNTABILITY AND PERFORMANCE

We talked about *accountability* as a component of character. It's also an important competency of performance management. Along with understanding expectations and follow-up, accountability is a core component of successful execution. When we understand what others expect as outcomes of our efforts and we feel a sense of personal responsibility to deliver on them, then there is potential for improved results.

As leaders, we help accountability by creating an architecture for it. One of the first things we do is outline individual accountabilities. This is about setting expectations. To be accountable, people need to understand what they are accountable *for*. What outcomes are they responsible for delivering? From the outset, metrics used to assess individual and team performance should also be clear. Why? So that your people can manage their actions from the very beginning to ensure they're aligned with goals.

Make sure to explain accountabilities and metrics during the interview process and reinforce it in onboarding. This helps weed out prospects who don't believe they're a match for the responsibilities of the role and/or are uncomfortable working in an accountability culture where metrics are used, performance is assessed, and consequences result. In this way, you boost performance further by only allowing accountable players onto the team.

When clarity is created, team members can better perform because they understand their position on the team and how the score is kept. Consider any sports team, for example. In football (soccer), the goalkeeper knows that their role is not to score goals but that it's to prevent them and they can use their hands to do so (within a certain area of the pitch). The striker knows they cannot use their hands to touch the ball at any time in carrying out their goal-scoring role. All team members know they have to work together to defend when they don't possess the ball. The coach provides clarity for each team member by describing the actions they should take individually, and at times in tandem with others, to produce a winning result.

Team performance lies where all individual performance areas overlap. It's a small area with a big impact. Ask any team member in sporting or military environments—where this thought process around teams is most apparent—and they will tell you that they all count on the person to the left and to the right of them to perform their roles, and when this is done well the result is victory.

In addition to creating clarity around accountability, leaders provide resources to support it. These may come in the form of standard operating procedures, checklists, information systems, and performance data. Team members are kept on the path toward success by allowing them reference tools that, when followed, deliver expected results.

Access to performance data also increases team member accountability. This provides the ability to compare individual and team performance to expected results and review gaps to determine how people may adjust their own actions in order to improve. When you regularly practice transparency and share performance data with team members, the result is greater mutual accountability. Team members feel obligated to one another, to themselves, and to the business.

Inspection is the third leg of the performance stool (understanding, ownership, follow-up). It not only supports good performance in its own right but also supports accountability. Follow-up signals to all that we're interested in progress and results. It shows that team members will be held accountable for efforts and outcomes and that performance has consequences. If no one is watching, then good performance can't be acknowledged or poor performance addressed.

Some individuals may also put in less than full effort (or no effort at all) to meet goals. For those team members whose sense of personal accountability isn't strong—or those who are accountable but have run up against obstacles and require help—the lack of follow-up signals that it's okay if individual expectations aren't met because no one cares enough to monitor for achievement. It's not okay, of course.

The heart of follow-up's relationship with accountability is feedback. You need to relay your follow-up findings to your people so they understand where they are in relation to your expectations. This sounds easy and like common sense, but it is less straightforward in practice. Leaders who don't engage in regular feedback conversations with their staff struggle at times. They may lack tact and ruin the relationship with insensitive, angry venting. Or they sugarcoat the feedback, failing to frankly explain their findings and concerns. Underperformers receive "satisfactory" appraisal ratings rather than having leaders sit down to have an important conversation with them. A trend toward central tendency occurs, with both the stars' and underperformers' gap in appraisal ratings, salary adjustments, and bonuses not being proportional to their true difference in performance levels. As a result, underperformers are encouraged to stay and overachievers become disheartened and move toward the exit door.

Whether driven by fear of the "uncomfortable" conversation, a desire to be liked, or a belief that feedback won't make a meaningful difference to performance, leaders who fail to provide critical feedback to staff lower the tone. It's been said that team culture is *the worst performance or behavior that you'll accept.* Feedback shows your people that you care enough to provide them information that will improve their performance and results.

Randy Pausch, in his moving video *The Last Lecture*, reminds us that our critics are the ones who still love and care about us precisely *because* they provide the feedback that stings. He tells us that when we make mistakes and we know it—and everyone else knows it and no one says a thing—that is a very lonely and perilous place to be. Why? Because it means they've already given up on you. Providing feedback is a core leadership responsibility.

You don't have to be an expert at everything to build and maintain a culture of accountability on your team. No one expects you to be omniscient (If you were, you wouldn't need a team!). The key is to be engaged enough with your direct reports to understand their core responsibilities and the main issues and challenges they face.

Finally, remember that you can delegate accountability for tasks and behaviors, but **you** own the performance of your team, collectively and individually. You don't get the option of throwing your staff under the bus and pointing the finger at them when things go wrong. You have to take ownership of the bad outcomes as well as the accolades. An executive I quite admire once said that as a leader it was his job to help put people up on stage "and whether they receive applause or tomatoes is up to them." I think the same is true of leaders themselves. Because they are always under the microscope and on stage, leaders have to brave the occasional well-aimed tomato if they are to gain the applause for themselves and their teams.

- ***Does each team member know the main accountabilities of their role and how success in the position will be measured?***
- ***Do you provide your team the resources to help maintain accountability, including standard operating procedures, checklists, technology, and performance data?***
- ***Do you use regular follow-up to help build and maintain accountability on your team?***

MOTIVATION AND PERFORMANCE

Excellence is where passion and talent collide. When our motivation is deep-seated and stems from longstanding interest that's connected to our life purpose, we push ourselves to the edge of our capabilities. We connect the joy, the pride in delivering excellence for a cause we hold dear, and the fulfillment of aligning our values, work, and talent together. It feels greatly rewarding. Why wouldn't it? There's no better feeling than performing at our very best for, and due to, a purpose we feel a deep personal connection to.

Without duplicating our exploration of motivation, it's obvious that the degree of motivation we feel to achieve a goal affects our performance. This is "will" versus "skill." No doubt, plenty of circumstances exist where we've felt capable of performing a task or reaching a goal successfully but just "didn't feel like it" and weren't motivated to act. It's not that we couldn't do something well, we just didn't want to.

Sometimes, leaders mistakenly hire team members who are perfectly capable of performing the role but have no real desire to do so because the position doesn't satisfy their internal motivators. Prospects take a job because they need the income, the job in order to fill out a spot on the resume', or "a foot in the door" so they can buy time to apply for the job they really want. This can result in unmotivated, disengaged staff that quickly leave after hire, resulting in substantial wasted time and money.

Whatever motivators you are leveraging, plainly indicate how rewards are earned. Teammates can then regulate their behavior and outcomes to achieve the desired incentives. Remember too that creativity needs to be utilized in providing rewards. Spending extra time with the boss at a work retreat may not be seen as a reward, but instead a burden of having to spend precious free time away from loved ones. Get to know your team well enough to understand what they will—and won't—see as a meaningful reward.

We often talk of "creating vision" as a leadership function, one which is vitally important during times of transition. The importance of creating and communicating vision to motivate staff and improve performance results is substantial. A leader with vision and values is often a significant reason staff stay in organizations. People want to have meaning and direction in their lives, in and outside of the workplace. Be the leader who provides it in the office—and possibly even helps people discover what they want outside of work—and you'll motivate your people to perform more to their potential.

As leaders, we're all salespeople to some degree. We regularly sell others on the need to adapt to changes or take action that meets corporate aims. In doing so, you must answer the "what's in it for me" question that lies within everyone if you're to create desire for action. If the stakes are high and the objective is important, you can't forget to engage minds *and* hearts along the way, or you and your people will underachieve. You've got to do it purposefully, as part of the process of performance planning.

As you enact plans and initiatives for employees to carry out in the field, remember that motivation is not a one-time exercise. As everyone encounters obstacles and unforeseen circumstances, self-doubt creeps in and motivation wanes. The regular discussions you schedule with staff reinvigorates them to perform. This is especially critical during important and/or lengthy initiatives to remind staff of the personal and professional benefits of good performance.

- *Do you try to ensure that each individual takes meaning from their work in order to motivate performance?*
- *Which motivators does each person find most fulfilling so that you can use them to drive achievement?*
- *Is your vision for the team well-communicated and appealing enough to the group to motivate performance?*
- *What activities to you undertake regularly to ensure you team's motivation to perform is sustained?*

EXPECTATIONS AND MEASURABLES

Performance management begins with understanding what performance looks like. What results are important? What outcomes are sought in terms of service, work products, quality, timeliness, etc.? What separates "good" from "bad" results? How will you know the difference? You will need to determine *what* results to focus on. Sometimes these are apparent based upon goals that have already been set for you and your team. They may also stem from your own review of strategic business goals and near-term operational objectives.

Past performance data is a good starting point as it indicates which goals the business believed were most important and how the organization and your team performed to them previously. You may or may not have latitude to determine what goals to set to support strategic organizational objectives. Whether you do or not, you should have an understanding of the organization's aims and how your team's work affects them. This provides meaning to the team's work.

When you set team objectives, consider their alignment with the company's larger goals. There's no sense setting expectations that don't contribute to the greater good somehow. You'll be wasting your people's time and resources and be ineffective in supporting the aims that your boss, and your boss' boss, believe are vital.

When choosing objectives, pay thought to whether you can accurately determine your degree of success in reaching them. If you can't quantify or otherwise apply metrics to the objective, it diminishes it as a performance management tool. Staff "try their best" without knowing whether it's resulted in acceptable performance. Performance is rationalized to be "successful" without any real basis, and the contribution to the organization's goals can't be measured or justified. Since what gets measured gets done, consider this factor in choosing your objectives.

Once you've chosen objectives, determine which supporting metrics will be most useful in gauging progress and achievement. Ideally the metrics will have benchmarks, so success can be determined against either past performance within the organization or some external standard. You can graphically represent objective metrics, which helps display trend data. You should also consider how easy it's going to be to gather and analyze information as well as the quality of the source data. There's little use choosing complex, hard-to-understand metrics that are so time-consuming to administer that the costs outweigh their benefits.

Weigh whether the metric chosen is the most meaningful measure of success for the objective. For instance, how do you measure improving the "quality of hires"? Is it some measure of productivity within the first year? Employee retention rates? Their place in a 9-box succession planning tool or some other measure of promotability? Is the best customer success measure for your organization revenue per customer? Customer retention? Products per customer? Numerous metric choices exist, particularly for broader areas such as financial or customer service goals. Make decisions regarding which metrics are the most vital and relevant in measuring progress and which are secondary. Only you can determine that based upon the context in which your organization operates. If you don't choose well, you'll end up placing important focus on unimportant activities.

Some words of caution about KPIs: Don't establish measurables if you don't intend to audit regularly to determine performance or share the results with those they affect. Periodically, I speak to leaders who indicate that some metric exists, established under a client service level agreement or other business imperative, that they intended to work to. Deadlines for responsiveness are one example. When I ask how often they audit internally against them to determine performance and how they're performing against the metrics, I'm periodically met with silence, a blank stare, or some vague answer that ad hoc customer feedback lets them know. This makes the exercise of choosing and documenting KPIs a waste of time and a frustrating one for stakeholders.

If the ability and intent to hold the team accountable for performance against metrics doesn't exist then don't use KPIs as they will serve no useful purpose. If you aren't going to gain, and use, knowledge about the performance of your business relative to the goals set, then don't attempt using metrics. You lose credibility with your employees, management, and customers when you commit to achievement efforts via KPIs in theory but not in practice.

If you do establish metrics and audit against them, don't keep the information to yourself as if it's a precious secret. Get information out to your people to create the sense of urgency and motivation to perform that makes a real difference to results. This also creates a culture of accountability and is the very foundation for performance.

Performance metrics, even if well-chosen and regularly measured, can be inappropriately applied in practice. In extreme cases, organizations have used a few objective metrics solely to determine pay raises, bonuses, eligibility for promotions, and performance appraisal results. This is a perversion of the idea of performance assessment, and obstinate organizations that insist on doing this risk alienating staff and plummeting morale as employees head for the door. It's also an emotionally unintelligent means of attempting to manage performance.

No one likes the sum total of their work contributions watered down to a handful of statistical metrics at the expense of the variety of ways they add value at work that can't easily be worked out on a calculator. With statistical measures only, how do you measure generally valued competencies— including those related to leadership potential (i.e., influencing, motivating, planning, follow-through, managing change, etc.)? How do you evaluate how well cultural values in the organization are upheld?

As much as people seek a fair process of evaluating their contributions and results, don't mistake this for their desire to be assessed via only objective metrics. The boss's opinion—and those of other stakeholders—do matter, and subjective evaluations based upon some defensible rationale are a valid part of the performance management process. Procedural fairness does not mean exclusive use of objective metrics. Plenty of ways, from purely subjective opinion to use of behavioral anchors and 360-degree evaluations, can be injected into performance management and still be viewed by others as fundamentally fair and appropriate.

Having set team goals and determined metrics for them, you should review how those goals will cascade down to the expectations you have for individual team members. It may be that the team goals translate directly into individual expectations in some cases, where a specific position may be responsible for one of the team goals, among others, that they are given. This may also require you to create specific goals distinct from the group goals themselves.

For instance, if the HR team goal is to decrease first year turnover by 10 percent, there may be metrics specific to the role of recruiter to ensure that good process is followed in making hiring decisions (i.e., random audit results on compliance with the hiring procedure) and ninety-day turnover is lowered. There may also be metrics for the training team related to compliance with onboarding procedures, new hire onboarding survey results, or six-month productivity metrics. For management staff, it could be an indicator of productivity of new hires in their roles during the first six or twelve months, as this could also be an indicator of hiring quality and potential for staff retention.

If you can, involve your staff in goal setting, choosing supporting metrics, and setting benchmarks for various levels of performance (meeting expectations, exceeding expectations, needs improvement, etc.). They'll be more committed to goal attainment if you do. In addition, they'll be more likely to understand how performance in their roles affects team objectives and how team goals in turn support the company's strategic aims.

Clearly form objectives and supporting metrics so they're concise and easy for team members to understand. Goal attainment is often tied to compensation adjustments and incentives. If staff views their goals as unreasonable and metrics as complex, they'll come to believe the system lacks fairness and transparency and that they are being taken advantage of. This won't bode well for their productivity, motivation, or retention.

Once you've clearly formed individual objectives and metrics, record them. This allows you to carefully review them and make adjustments. In addition, set the benchmarks for performance within the metrics, including what constitutes meeting expectations, exceeding them, and falling short. For statistical measures, this is the "scorecard" you use to keep track of progress and results. Not all goals will be statistically based, and for the others you'll need to be clear about the quality and timeliness of the work products you expect. Using behavioral anchors—describing behaviors that demonstrate what falling short of, meeting, or exceeding expectations are—will help you.

Once you've documented the individual objectives and supporting metrics, communicate them to the team. Individual discussions are ideal because any role-specific questions or concerns can be addressed. Make sure each team member receives a copy of the documented objectives and metrics they're accountable for. Record the goals and metrics in your HR information system, annual performance appraisal document, or other tool if you can too. Staff view verbal goals with the healthy skepticism they deserve as memories may easily fade, minds can be changed, and disagreement over wording and translation can arise. Documentation produces increased mutual commitment, trust and clarity.

When you communicate goals and metrics, pay thought to the "why" of the conversation. Team members will want to understand the reasons the objectives should be important to them. They need to see the benefit to themselves, the team, and the organization. This speaks to motivation, which we've already discussed. If a team member is looking for the next promotion, to expand their skills further, deliver excellent service to customers, or feel valued, explain the connection between those drivers and reaching the objectives set for them.

Another word on goal setting and communication: Nothing undermines this process more than the lack of timeliness. Both your credibility and the company's are damaged, for instance, when goals for the calendar year are rolled out in February or March, by which time a number of weeks have passed by without clear direction that allows staff to focus their performance efforts. Staff view this lost time with skepticism, particularly when stretch goals are applied that puts them further behind in meeting their goals. If you can't deliver goals and metrics on time to your people, consider adjusting the measurement period (i.e., March to March) so that you can.

- *Do you review available historic information to help determine what, and what level of, goals are appropriate for your team and its members?*
- *How do you ensure today that the KPIs you choose are the most appropriate indicators to support achievement of company objectives?*
- *Do you make appropriate use of objective and subjective goals set for team members?*
- *Do you clearly document the goals and KPIs set so your team members have a reference tool and are clear about how success will be measured?*
- *Do you try to connect the goals to individual motivators to help drive performance?*

YOU HAVE TO INSPECT WHAT YOU EXPECT

Consistent follow-up is probably the most common performance management shortcoming among leaders. Commonly rationalized by statements such as "I haven't got time to follow up with everyone," "I don't want to micromanage," or "I trust my people know what they're doing," some leaders will neglect to carry through on plans by overlooking follow-up. They're then surprised by their staff's failure to meet deadlines, deliver intended work products, or progress past the first obstacle they encounter. Projects remain incomplete, and business progress is negatively affected. Clients are disappointed and complain or leave, and the reputation of the team and company are damaged. Leaders could have avoided some or all of these negative consequences if they had taken the time to steer their ship away from the rocky waters of underperformance.

The Hawthorne Effect is well known in scientific circles; it's the phenomenon whereby individuals change their behavior *because* they are being observed. This is, to an extent at least, the whole point of follow-up. People change their actions because they understand that critical comments will follow—and from that, follow-up consequences naturally arise. People then become conditioned to apply full effort whether they're being observed or not because they understand that they *may* be at some point. They may be asked to account for their efforts and results. They come to understand that the accounting matters.

It's worth mentioning that unless consequences do follow there's little point in following up. If you do not take up opportunities to recognize and reward strong efforts and results and don't address underperformance, then the exercise just wastes everyone's time and erodes your credibility as leader. When you turn over a rock, you've got to be prepared to deal with what's beneath it.

Most crucially, when you follow up you gain the ability to assess progress against expected results and determine whether you're on track to meet goals. It informs your subsequent actions as a leader, either to encourage more of the same because you're on track to achieve/overachieve or adjust the team's behavior due to underperformance. There may be changed circumstances in the field, unknown internal constraints, or external factors that require you and your people to adjust course. Without checking in periodically, you may continue down a path that diverges further from goal attainment rather than realigns with it.

When regular follow-up occurs, so does the opportunity to provide performance coaching. Leaders have a wonderful opportunity to engage in conversations that help their people carry out their roles more successfully. You have the chance to understand how your people approach their jobs and ask questions to help them uncover alternative courses of action. You can provide feedback, share your experience of negotiating through similar situations, and direct staff to other sources of knowledge.

A reality I've consistently relayed to leaders at all levels is that your people either see you as an obstacle or a resource on their way to fulfillment and success at work. Performance coaching helps you act as the latter for your team. You unearth the obstacles to performance for them, and help remove the obstacles or find ways for your people to transcend them. This shows your people that you "have their back" and will support them any way you can on their road to achievement.

Follow-up activities won't be universally well-received. Some team members may resent inspection as a signal that you do not trust them. It will take some time to get them to understand that a "trust but verify" culture means that you inspect not only to ensure results but also to coach and provide resources necessary to support their success. Those that balk at inspection on the basis that it's a distraction from them doing their "real work" will come to acknowledge that part of their role is reporting on progress, obstacles encountered, and additional resource needs. These are contributions that go beyond their typical task work and are valuable to us as leaders and to the team.

Follow-up is a normal part of building healthy accountability, coaching, and removing obstacles to success. You neglect your organization's and team's needs when you fail to follow up. Inspection doesn't have to be at the expense of good working relationships with your people—in fact, it helps us build healthier, productive working relationships when follow-up discussions are woven into the fabric of performance management. Done well, your people will come to cherish the time you spend on follow-up because they'll have learned that you do so for their benefit as well as for the team's.

- *Do you build in regular follow-up to the process of managing performance of your people?*
- *In your eyes, how often is "regular" follow-up with individuals and the team as a whole?*
- *Do you coach and remove obstacles to performance during follow-up conversations?*
- *Do you hold team members accountable for performance and behavior issues during follow-up; do consequences result?*

THE ROLE OF RECOGNITION AND REWARD

Recognition and reward is a common employee motivation and performance management practice that encourages productive behavior. Often, employee engagement surveys highlight this as an area of opportunity for companies, and there's an enduring relationship between recognition and reward, motivation, and performance results. Remember, too, the perils of over-reliance on external reward in motivating performance and retaining staff.

It's important to understand the factors of size and duration when applying rewards for your staff. Rewards must be seen as meaningful enough to be worth the effort and trouble of the journey. Each day, we all do cost/ benefit analyses to determine if we're going to take action. Is it worth the effort to get up from the couch to make that cup of coffee? To make the crowded commute in to work? To take the car in for servicing on time? To do the gardening? Only we know the answers to those questions. If we decide that the reward (often related to either seeking pleasure or avoiding pain) is worth more than the price we're going to pay in order to achieve it then we undertake action.

If you offer scant reward for initiatives that require considerable effort, you may do more damage than offering none at all. Staff may be insulted, feel you're taking advantage of them, and view the organization as lacking real appreciation for their people. You have to weigh the scale of the reward and the amount of the effort taken to achieve it in order to determine the appropriate size of the prize.

There's also the appeal of immediacy in reward initiatives to consider. If the effort is going to be time consuming and the reward provided only after months or even year(s), then the size of the reward needs to increase to compensate for the delay. Small rewards dangled a year out are diminished in appeal as staff may view it as so far off to be worthless as a motivation and reward tool. If staff can no longer envision the reward from a distance, then they're unlikely to take steps toward it. Remember that out of sight equals out of mind.

The resources and means to recognize and reward performance vary based upon your operating environment, however the basic premises are universal. Our discussion on motivation outlined common types of internal and external motivators, and these are intimately connected to recognition and reward. The first step? Understanding what motivates your people individually. To what extent are externally driven motivators of value? What internal motivators are important? This informs how we apply recognition and reward to each person's unique circumstances. The type and mix of tools we apply can make all the difference to our team members' feelings of appreciation.

Motivators for performance are commonly treated as distinct from recognition and reward tools. This is a mistake. The motivators to perform typically *are* the rewards for that very performance. If they're external, our team member must wait for us to give them out. If they're internal, they're provided as a part of performing the work itself. Internal or external, the motivators that passionately drive an individual become the most powerful reward for achievement itself. Know them well and you'll not only be better prepared to drive performance but also more adept at recognizing and rewarding success.

Numerous studies assert that compensation and benefits are not the top reasons employees remain in organizations. External rewards and motivators are commodities that the competition can easily duplicate. Other companies can easily replicate base compensation, incentive schemes, spot bonuses, gifts, benefits, and the like to potentially offer a more attractive "deal" for staff members.

The lack of perceived fairness or competitiveness of base pay may affect employee engagement and retention, however increased pay alone is likely to have minimal effect on retention. Pay alone, as long as it's viewed as fundamentally fair, is a less powerful driver of motivation, performance, and retention in general than other means. There's a subset of staff for which compensation is the overriding motivator and valued reward, but don't make the mistake of applying that principle to all your people as the default. You might be spending money unnecessarily when other forms of recognition and reward are actually seen as more meaningful.

If compensation isn't the primary motivator or potential reward mechanism for most staff, then what is? Well that answer is, of course, not so simple as both are individually-based. Consider some of the main themes of reward, however. The first is simple, cost-effective, and you can implement it yourself today. It's praise. Many teammates place a premium value on spontaneous verbal praise from their direct supervisor. It lifts people's spirits and supports self-esteem. It encourages us, validates our worth, and can boost effort and results.

When you give praise in public, you encourage behavioral modeling and boost its power even further. You can also supercharge the value of praise by putting it in writing. Handwritten thank you cards dropped on a desk or mailed to your team member's home address are appreciated. I had one coworker, a senior executive, who demonstrated how much this was cherished as he kept a handwritten thank you card in his briefcase that someone gave to him more than ten years earlier. He remembered to "pay it forward," and regularly gave his people handwritten notes of thanks and praise, which I'm sure left an indelible mark on them.

Peer recognition can be as meaningful as that from management, and creating a culture of praise within your team is important. If the praise is genuine and spontaneous, when it comes from a coworker our work feels even more validated and our desire to continue to perform rises.

Symbolism is another tool for recognition and reward. This may be in the form of "Top Performer," "Special Contributor," or other awards given to individuals and teams. When you provide a tangible symbol of appreciation, a strong memory of recognition follows for your people. It's a powerful means of supporting culture and performance aims, as the deeds we choose to celebrate indicate what we hold as valuable on the team.

An additional recognition and reward tool is also simple and easy to implement today: It's giving of your time. When you take time with your people, you demonstrate your commitment to their development and success. You signal to others that they matter and are worth spending your precious limited resources on. We crave time and attention from people whom we respect, can help us, and have positive relationships with. If your relationships with your people are on solid ground, you can use your time and attention as a positive recognition and reward tool.

Spend your time and attention on those who desire to be coached, developed, and validated. These are resources that you and you alone control. There's no budget approval process, no paperwork to fill out, and no approval chain in order to spend time and attention. And while your budget of time and attention is limited, it means you get to think carefully about how you spend it for maximum impact.

When a team member's motivation is continual learning and development, the process itself of gaining knowledge—whether you or someone else is the source—is the reward. Few of us want to remain in a position where the opportunity to learn new skills and gain knowledge isn't a part of the work experience. Even if individuals have no aspirations to move beyond their current role, they want to learn how to be more effective performing it and support others well. For those who seek continual development, learning becomes the reward.

Leaders often overlook the use of delegation, autonomy, and trust as forms of recognition and reward. Think about the last time your own boss demonstrated their trust in you or verbalized it to your peer group. I bet it felt good. It's nice to know that others feel we can be relied upon and can be given the freedom to take responsibility and make decisions. After all, that's how we hone our critical thinking and decision-making skills—by practicing them.

Demonstrate your trust in your people, delegate additional responsibility and authority to them, and allow them more freedom to make choices on their own. These acts recognize their expertise, reliability, and your faith in them. The job becomes more complex, more challenging, and more their own. We all seek to control our destiny and results at work, and for many of us this motivates performance and makes our position more fulfilling.

Ultimately, a variety of resources are available to you to motivate, recognize, and reward performance, but you have to unearth them through understanding your people. Learning motivation and reward preferences means building individual relationships with team members. We all crave healthy individual relationships in our lives, including a positive, productive one with our boss. When our manager personally gets to know and understand us, and to learn about our aspirations and needs, he or she sends the message that we matter. This feels good, and why would you leave a supervisor that feels good to work with? We need people if we're to manage performance as a leader—and it's nice when the good ones stay with us.

- *What are each of your team members' recognition and reward preferences?*
- *Do you over-rely on monetary (compensation, bonuses) and nonmonetary external rewards (prizes, gifts) to drive performance?*
- *How often do you use other forms of reward such as time and attention, learning and development, autonomy, praise and affirmation, and symbolism such as trophies and certificates?*
- *Do you regularly take up opportunities to praise your team members publicly and in one-on-one conversation, or is your praise very hard to come by?*

HIRING AND ONBOARDING'S
RELATIONSHIP TO PERFORMANCE

A variety of leadership resources are already available to you, or you can easily build and maintain them. You are the minder of this toolbox. If you choose not to gather and actively use resources for performance management, then you neglect the primary reason that managers exist in the first place. Remember again that a manager's role is to gain results through others' efforts. Leaders regularly commit fundamental attribution error—believing that the sole source of underperformance is their team member rather than the environment (including systems, processes, resources, and the leader's own shortcomings). You have to look beyond the employee and also create an atmosphere that's conducive to success. Remove roadblocks and be the resource that helps your people achieve, and you will justify your leadership role well.

The first performance management tool is the hiring process itself. Do you have a structured process for recruitment and selection of staff members, including job descriptions, structured screening and interview questionnaires, pre-employment assessments, candidate rating and selection discussions, and background checks? The chances of being a successful leader increase with the talent and potential of your team members. Work to minimize the chances of a mis-hire. Maximize the chances that you've got a good basic fit between the company, position, and individual by structuring the interview and selection process, and you'll have greater potential to perform well.

I can't emphasize enough how important this is and how commonly supervisors neglect to take hiring seriously enough, viewing it as an unwelcome distraction from the day job. Some believe they must quickly attend to hiring so that the seat gets filled with someone—anyone—who can come in and "hit the ground running." Recruitment isn't a distraction from your main duties. As a leader, *it is* one of your main duties. This isn't something you can, or should, delegate to someone else. It's your team, so treat those seats on it as a precious commodity.

With your new team member during onboarding, you should explicitly discuss the job description, KPIs, behavior and productivity expectations, available resources, and work deliverables and deadlines. Your relationship is more productive when both parties know the expectations of each other, how performance is measured, and what information is available to compare performance to expectations.

- *Do you treat hiring effectively as the first step in managing the performance of your team?*
- *Do you consider recruitment and onboarding activities an important part of managing performance on your team?*
- *Do you discuss performance issues, measurables, and expectations promptly when new team members onboard?*

PERFORMANCE COMMUNICATION

A simple but crucial tool you have to manage performance are regular staff meetings. Determine the cadence of these meetings, with them happening more frequently where the work environment is dynamic or underperformance is an issue. For example, in short-cycle sales or recruitment roles, meetings may need to be more frequent to review past performance, update current activity and changing work priorities, and predict the future pipeline of work and revenue. Control the activity, and you can control results. When the activity changes more frequently, so does the need for meetings. With new staff settling into their roles or others struggling with performance, the need for more frequent discussions allows your time with your people to be spent where it is most impactful.

Remember that everything you do—or don't do—sends a message to new staff, who are particularly impressionable during the first few months of their employment. Invest in them through regular performance discussions and you'll find you will have to meet less over time. Likewise, holding discussions more often with underperformers signals to them that you're supportive but also holding them accountable for improvement.

Once you've set a regular cadence to your meetings, make effective use of the time you are setting aside to conduct them. What will the purpose and agenda be? How will you need to prepare? What information must you gather and share? What action items should result from discussions? Treat these meetings like any other; prepare for them and set an agenda so that they're a productive use of everyone's time.

The advantage of having staff gather up performance data relevant to their own role before meetings is that they get to know it well. It becomes part of your team's culture to "understand the numbers" and self-audit performance so that achievement is regularly on their minds. If this can't be done and you have to present the data to your people, make sure it occurs prior to the meeting so that all are prepared to speak to results intelligently. If results are good, celebrate and acknowledge effort. If results are not so good, your people need to know so they can help right the ship. No one can correct a problem they don't know exists, so create urgency through greater performance transparency. If they know it, they can own it.

Make sure discussions are two-way and interactive. Find out if your team members want to cover any other issues before the meeting so that you can prepare yourself properly. In addition, talk to them about progress and successes. These meetings are a tool for performance management, and talking to your people about their past successes and highlights is food for the soul. You're on a regular schedule of meetings now, so you have regular chances to use the power of recognition and reward to positively influence performance.

As a part of the conversation you also should review progress against plans, goals, and set deadlines. Did your team member fully accomplish them? If not, where are the gaps and what got in the way of reaching expectations? Ask for input so that you can better understand how they spent their time and effort and what problems, from their perspective, they encountered along the way.

Where performance shortfalls occur you need to address them, as this is the heart of building accountability and a culture of performance. Were the problems based on skill or will? Did your team member have the knowledge and expertise to accomplish the tasks? Did some environmental or motivational factors get in the way of accomplishment? If not, then you have a coaching opportunity around execution. If effort was strong but results did not follow, look to skill development to increase effectiveness.

As an example, it's common to use tools like yield pyramids in revenue-generating roles where sales staff are required to make calls, gain contacts, schedule appointments, obtain opportunities to bid for business, and win business of some average revenue amount. If you have activity data you can predict, with some degree of accuracy, how much effort it takes to gain results. If team members make many calls but gain few contacts, the ratio of calls/contacts is low and you can ask questions to determine whether they used the right means and times to gain contact. If contact/appointment setting ratios are low, then you can examine the content of the conversations salespeople have with prospects. For each step up the pyramid a ratio exists, and if effort is present but results don't follow, you can coach for performance to increase the ratios by increasing your people's expertise.

If the amount of activity or effort doesn't appear to exist, then the core of the problem is motivation or time usage. This is about first controlling the *amount* of activity to control results. Once that occurs, you can move on to review the effectiveness of the activity itself. When motivation appears to wane, re-establishing clear connections between your people's professional desires and performance results is important. Time usage and prioritization discussions require you to help your team member concentrate on the most important and productive uses of time and effort during the day. This is a conversation around focus and is another important function of your individual staff meetings.

During regularly scheduled performance conversations, listen to your team member's view on the support they need to accomplish goals. Part of this conversation is a voyage of discovery to gain greater understanding of the issues, obstacles, and activities that are *actually* occurring out in the field. Our belief in how our people undertake their work each day and reality always diverge somehow.

When it comes to performance and behavior, you'll often hear this saying from human resource professionals: "Document, document, document!" Have a mechanism for documenting the discussions you have around performance and behavior, and not just in the cases where a problem occurs. Performance documents exist to proactively manage performance so that the chances of underperformance itself decrease and the odds of success increase. This is because clarity and focus are created.

Summarize the conversation in writing and share the information with your team member. They'll appreciate the reference tool which will help them remember their progress and accomplishments, plans of action to meet performance expectations, and the commitments you have both made to support future results. This creates accountability for both you and your team members.

You'd be surprised how many times I've asked leaders about the promises they made only to hear that they'd like to fire a team member they failed to help in any way as they had documented previously. The document is a performance management tool, not just for the employee but for you as a leader too. Regular meetings with documented summaries help your people understand their progress and results throughout the year. Don't rely on vague recollections in the hope that both you and your people mutually understand performance expectations and results over the course of the year when it comes time to complete formal appraisal processes.

If you do choose to have "Quarterly Performance Review" meetings or something similar with your leadership group, be sure the primary purpose of these discussions is benign. I have seen organizations using these meetings to publicly shame leaders struggling with performance, crucifying them in front of their peers. It's embarrassing and shameful for the executives that allow it to happen and perpetuates an unhealthy culture of blame. When management allows this to occur, knocking others down to lift themselves up, they confirm the fragility of their own egos. They evidence their own failure to look in the mirror and truly "own" the performance of the people who report to them—which is exactly what they're tell their subordinates to do.

- *Do you currently have regular one-on-one and group meetings set with your team?*
- *Are meetings structured and do they have an agenda, including assessing progress, results, and recognizing effort?*

- *Do these meetings contain dialogue, with your people sharing their thoughts and concerns, and information about the resources and support they need in order to succeed?*
- *Are periodic meetings documented somehow so that you and your team members can reference them to help with performance and prepare for future meetings?*

←——————————————————

FORMAL PERFORMANCE MANAGEMENT PROCESSES

Your people's expectation is that they progress at work—whether related to pay, rewards, position, title, skills, experience, credibility, or other factors. The performance appraisal is a common tool for assessing progress and performance against expectations. Part of the performance appraisal process is indeed to assess past performance against set expectations. Were skill, credibility, experience, and competence evidenced via results, including performance growth versus prior years?

Our assessments of our people affect their base and variable compensation, opportunities for job changes and promotion, and the allocation of additional duties with broader scope and impact. Position, power, punishment, and prizes are common outcomes of the performance appraisal process. The opportunity to acknowledge progress and achievement exists, just as in any other follow-up process.

If you're assessing against statistically based performance metrics, the process is normally straightforward. Results fall into a range that is benchmarked against some rating scale, and the employee is rated accordingly. There's often a weight attached to each metric (i.e., the results count 10 percent toward the overall performance rating). The same process applies to the assessment of subjective metrics such as competency ratings (i.e., goal-oriented, organization skills, customer focus, etc.) or ratings of how well the employee's behavior reflects the company's core values (i.e., integrity, accountability, teamwork, etc.). It's useful to have behavioral anchors set out for subjective metrics describing, for example, what types of behavior constitute "outstanding" and which demonstrate "needs improvement." Provide specifics in justifying ratings that are subjective so others may view the process as rational and fair.

Don't let people walk away feeling the assessment process was arbitrary because you failed to come to the table with examples and specifics. You diminish the value of the performance assessment when you do this, and your staff loses respect for you because you haven't put in the effort to support a meaningful conversation using what, in most cases, is a once-a-year process.

In addition to the backward-looking aspects of performance appraisal processes, future performance is impacted by setting goals and measurables, creating action plans and outlining support resources, and discussing agendas for professional development that enhance skills and experience. The performance appraisal is the primary tool for goal setting and outlining performance measurables for the upcoming period in order to focus efforts.

Staff understand the need to perform and reach expectations. What they hunger to know is *how* to achieve. Well-constructed performance appraisals include enough detail around action plans so that the main factors supporting performance are clear. This includes the behaviors, plans, deadlines, and support resources that will help goal attainment. In addition to operational goals, also outline the goals for professional development for the year and the plans and resources that will support those aims. It takes time to create effective performance appraisals, but you should ensure that you're fully utilizing this important tool to influence performance.

- *Do you provide detailed information and examples in support of your appraisal ratings to help your people understand how you view their performance?*
- *Do you use performance appraisals to manage current and future performance by setting goals, including KPIs, and outlining aims for learning and development?*

MENTORING AND 360-DEGREE REVIEW PROCESSES

Mentoring programs are usually formal, where the processes of orienting mentors to the program and its administration are structured. Mentoring is a common resource for onboarding new team members during the first several months of employment. Mentors are also used to develop leaders and high potentials, aiding their performance. Experienced, well-performing peers or those in higher-level positions often mentor team members.

Formal programs commonly use documents to guide and record the periodic meetings that take place, and help alert others to issues that arise in order to provide mentees additional support. The mentor practices their counseling, problem resolution, and coaching skills too—and this can also positively impact their own current and future performance.

If you do choose to formalize your mentoring process, make sure it's easy to implement and administer. Complicated, time-consuming, and painful to complete processes have led to the death of many well-intentioned employee initiatives. It's much better to do five things well than try to be the master of twenty-five tasks. Make the process, format, and supporting documents easy to complete and track. Try to measure the impact of such programs, relating them to decreases in time-to-productivity for new staff, overall productivity, retention, or internal promotion rates to prove the value of the program and maintain support for it.

If you're looking to implement mentoring in your team, however, don't worry about all that. You can make a positive impact for your people, in addition to the networking and cultural integration benefits of mentoring. If the program spreads within the organization, others can further analyze its effect in time. Don't try to boil the ocean at this point. If mentoring seems like it could positively impact individual performance, then consider implementing it. It can be informal initially and become more structured over time if needed.

Another useful performance management resource is the 360-degree feedback process. This is less familiar than mentoring, but is also a powerful tool for accelerating individual performance. Providing diverse, holistic feedback about performance and behavior can help team members focus their performance and development efforts. By gathering and providing feedback from a variety of stakeholders (peers, managers, subordinates, internal customers, external customers, etc.) a more complete picture of performance and behavior is available to your people for review.

People must have courage to subject themselves to the 360-degree feedback process, as they receive feedback from a variety of stakeholders and not all of it will be positive. That's the point, after all. The feedback that stings is typically the most useful to professional development. The value of such programs is also in the ability to highlight strengths that should be maximized in current and future positions. Additionally, blind spots may be uncovered where behaviors are inhibiting performance.

People interact with us based on how they perceive us—not how we want them to perceive us. If we want to improve our results, we need to change others' perceptions that inhibit performance and relationship building. We do that by changing *our own* thoughts and behavior. The 360-degree feedback process allows us to view ourselves through others' eyes, and we may not like what we see. It takes courage to face this, but the potential acceleration of performance and professional development is more than worth it.

Some executives pay external coaches large amounts of money to provide them the same feedback they consistently ignore from the people already working with them. It's the irony of the industry that many executive coaches will acknowledge—that they get fired periodically for holding a mirror up to some senior leaders who don't like what they see and can't take ownership of their own behavior. All those who use the 360-degree feedback process need to come into it with an open mind.

Numerous third-party companies have created templates and processes for 360-degree feedback, and program administration can be outsourced to them if needed. At its most basic level, leaders can simply gather feedback from stakeholders—with the team member's knowledge that the process is happening—and provide a summary to the employee themselves. It doesn't have to be complicated. Follow-up is the key here.

- *Do you take advantage of others' expertise in the business, using them to mentor your people?*
- *Do you gather information from a variety of stakeholders about your people's performance and behavior to use in 360-degree assessment initiatives or performance appraisals?*

POLICIES, PROCEDURES, WORKFLOWS, AND PROCESS MAPS

Policies and procedures can help your people obtain better, more consistent results. These are the "instruction manuals" to guide their behavior and meet expectations. They can also be valuable in ensuring that law, regulation, and service level agreements are followed. We've discussed how critical setting and communicating expectations are to performance. Clearly documented policies and procedures are an integral part of this. When you provide updated, clear, and easy-to-follow guides for behavior, you're helping to control the actions that control results.

If you've ever tried to put together an item without the directions, you likely found the experience more stressful, time consuming, and ineffective than it needed to be. Sometimes you got lucky, and it all turned out okay. More than likely, however, you realized you put the parts together wrong because you operated through trial and error and had to spend time correcting mistakes. You wasted valuable time and effort to come up with something that *looks* like the picture on the box. It may hold together over time—or may not.

Why subject your team members to this trial and error process, leaving them to stumble along rather than providing them a roadmap to make the journey easier? There's a reason recipes are used in cooking. No one shows up at a chain restaurant hoping that their favorite dish looks and tastes completely different than it did at the location down the road. There's comfort in familiarity and consistency for customers and coworkers. The predictability of results is part of what customers purchase, so provide your people the recipe to make it happen.

If successful execution is based on clarity, and clarity is based on simplicity, then make your policies and procedures easy to follow. Don't write a novel; no one will read or follow it. Periodically audit your policies and procedures too. We all know that changing circumstances with clients, legal environments, technology, and business operations can render policies and procedures obsolete. Put them on an audit cycle so that you review them at least annually to ensure they're still relevant and up to date. Assign more than one person to attempt to follow the procedure during the audit process, including someone who is less familiar with the job it pertains to. The ultimate test of a procedure's effectiveness is a novice's ability to obtain a successful outcome by following it. If you win the lottery tomorrow and quickly retire to a beach somewhere, could your (former) coworkers continue to perform well because of your policies and procedures? Tribal knowledge is the enemy of consistent and successful performance. You don't need to get every task, no matter how menial, documented. If you want repeatable results on the important stuff, however, get it down on paper.

- *Do you provide enough guidance for your people today through the creation and use of policies, procedures, process maps, and workflow diagrams?*
- *Do you periodically audit these tools to ensure they're still relevant and do not need updating or discarding?*

DEALING WITH UNDERPERFORMANCE

When team members fall short of expectations, we need to consider a number of factors in order to successfully address performance problems. The first is our own role in the outcome. It's common for leaders to mistakenly assume that the root of the problem lies entirely within the team member.

Effective leaders look in the mirror first before they turn it upon others. Examine your own responsibility in results that fall short. Explore whether you created enough understanding in your people for them to meet their performance aims.

Were expectations simple and clear? Did you document them to provide staff reference points as they undertook their work? Were KPIs established and data about progress regularly supplied to your people? Were the resources available to help your team members made clear to them, including procedures and systems? Did staff know where, and when, to go for help if they encountered obstacles? Did you effectively communicate all this information and check to confirm that staff understood it? All of these issues can affect execution, and if you failed here you likely produced underperformance in your team members.

Having looked to yourself, you also need to review environmental impacts on performance. Reviewing systems, procedures, reporting structures, communication flows, and resource provision may also lead to the conclusion that you need to further adjust the environment to better support performance. Clear the path of rocks and fallen trees to create an easier route to success for your people.

Having reviewed these factors, you also need to explore how your team members themselves, via their own actions and behavior, contributed to the problem. They certainly own a piece of the responsibility for their performance, and it may be a big one. This is where the "skill versus will" examination comes in and where you adjust your coaching and training to meet the specific needs you've uncovered.

The discovery process is not one-way. You and your team member need to be actively engaged in conversation about performance and keenly interested in resolving the causes of underperformance together. You can't be more invested in this process than your people are. The general philosophy is to focus on facts, including actions and behaviors. When discussions about performance issues arise, don't make a summary judgment about the personal characteristics of others (he's rude, careless; she's lazy, unfeeling). Separate the people from the problem to avoid personally offending and damaging the relationship.

Speak to what is seen and heard. Use facts, examples, and data. Talk about what you've concluded from your observations and the potential negative consequences if you're correct (Don't treat your conclusions as fact, though. There's usually more to the story). Allow your team member to share their own story and potential reasons behind the performance issues. Having explored both sides of the story, you'll then need to produce some alternative solutions in order to improve performance. Both parties must be committed once they've agreed on a solution.

You have an audience, beyond your underperforming team member, who will be keenly interested in whether you make a good-faith effort to manage up or are merely laying the groundwork for sending someone to the unemployment line. Team members will be acutely sensitive to the culture you're building around performance through your actions.

No one likes to be blindsided by managers who, lacking the courage to directly address performance or behavior issues informally, hide behind the formal process of the "performance improvement plan." Such leaders abdicate responsibility away from themselves to "the process" and lose the respect of many when they do.

When a problem arises, unless it's severe enough to warrant immediate formal corrective action, start with informal means such as verbal counseling. This doesn't mean that conversations are less robust, only that the approach takes a more casual tone with a focus on coaching performance. You should still document a summary of the conversation and date it so that you have a record of prior attempts to address performance. Don't let the first conversation about performance problems be a formal "note to the file" unless it is absolutely warranted. Think how you'd feel if you were in your team member's shoes and the first performance discussion included a written warning. You'd likely feel angry, surprised, and betrayed, among other things.

Whatever processes your organization uses to address people problems, deal promptly with performance and behavioral issues once you identify them. When you fail to do so, you set a low bar as the acceptable standard on your team and build a culture where performance and accountability are only paid lip service to. High performers see that their superior results aren't differentiated from low performers, and low performers aren't held accountable for improving their own results. If you're a high performer in a team environment where you end up working tirelessly to compensate for the failings of others, that doesn't feel very good. Pretty soon you start looking for a different environment where you can shine brighter.

Let's be clear though: No one likes being unsuccessful and repeatedly failing to meet the expectations set for them. When you neglect to address performance or behavior problems, they send a message that your expectations have sunk lower. When that happens, a mindset shift occurs among your team members. Individuals feel less concern, guilt, or accountability for what once was a standard of underperformance but clearly is now acceptable because of your inaction.

I once observed a particular region in a company underperforming against their primary measurables. When my colleagues and I dug deeper, we found a pattern of neglect by leaders to address performance and behavior issues. Coming in late to work or not complying with your schedule was acceptable. So was failing to undertake the volume and quality of activity needed to reach goals. When results failed to follow efforts, no one was being held to account. In the end, this was a culture created by leadership in the region that was the ultimate responsibility of the senior regional manager. What happened as a result? The organization started by addressing the primary performance issue in the region—and found a new regional senior manager. If you're a leader, you own the outcomes of all those that report to you, directly or indirectly. If you fail to hold others accountable for improvements, then you become the problem rather than the solution.

- *Do you promptly address underperformance, to both help your struggling team member and send a message to all your people that they'll be held accountable for their results?*
- *Do you start by addressing underperformance directly and informally, or do you hide behind formal process and the "performance improvement plan" or written warning process?*
- *Do you address underperformance rationally as a problem-solving exercise, coming prepared with facts and examples of underperformance when holding discussions with team members?*

Section 5

SERVANCY AND STEWARDSHIP

T he concepts of *servancy* and *stewardship* are relatively new to leadership philosophy. While *servancy* has some facets in common with *character*, particularly humility, compassion, forgiveness, and self-awareness, there are also other traits servant leaders possess. What is *servant leadership*, however? Let's first describe what it is *not*. Servant leadership is not a weakened form of leadership. It's not a boundaryless form of management that eschews standards, principles, or structure. It doesn't abdicate responsibility for efforts and outcomes away from leaders, and it doesn't accept lower standards of behavior or work products. It doesn't advocate away from high accountability or consistent results.

Servant leaders understand that along with the responsibility of providing purpose and direction comes the obligation to be an important resource for goal fulfillment. It's an actively engaged way of leading that doesn't just sit back and issue pronouncements. The primary role such leaders play is that of *provider*. They obtain resources, clear the pathway, and allow others the latitude to apply their expertise. They don't sit on a pedestal above the group, speaking idly about how they have teammates instead of subordinates. They walk the walk.

Servant leaders understand that they don't "own" anything in their organization. They realize they've been entrusted with a duty of care for the organization's resources, and foremost among them is the people on their teams. They accept that either they or others are only "passing through" and intersect for a time because circumstances warrant it. They look at leadership through a different lens and think about legacy. All leaders leave one. You and I forever remember the leaders who have taught us pivotal lessons through their kindness or cruelty, compassion or insensitivity, inspiration or demotivation, and courage or cowardice.

Servant leadership is intimately linked to character. It's a character-based philosophy of leadership that can be particularly powerful when leaders align character with action in a way that supports group achievement. It also *feels* good, because it's authentic. Leadership becomes a true expression of ourselves and because of this emotional energy isn't burned maintaining facades and acting the part.

It's important to understand that just being authentically aligned to our character, values, and beliefs isn't enough. Just as we've mentioned that "masks" of leadership become obsolete, you can't assume servant leadership if you don't share the character traits necessary to operate successfully in the role. If you are "in it to win it" just for yourself and view people as an expendable resource like any other, you won't succeed as a servant leader.

You cannot assume servant leadership as a guise just because it sounds like "good business" and you don't really believe in its underlying foundation. We've all probably witnessed self-centered egotists with an intellectual superiority complex try to adopt servant leadership, or at least decide to tolerate it in subordinate leaders. People smell the insincerity in them, and their act never lasts for long. In the end, they revert back to their default leadership style because character is never content until it's expressed. It's exactly for that reason that servant leadership can be such a powerful tool, and this is also why the pretenders can't adopt it as a philosophy on a whim.

You don't take a course on servant leadership and decide it's for you. Instead, you discover whether your personal beliefs, values, and characteristics align with it. A lack of humility, empathy, selflessness, interest in developing others, and willingness to empower—together with a sense of superiority, a focus just on numbers, and a transactional style of leading—means you're unlikely to ever even explore whether servant leadership will work for you. That's okay, because it won't.

Servant leadership warrants attention, however, because it's aligned with the leadership needs and preferences of most team members in today's workplace. It can, indeed, be "good business." It's important to also remember that servant leadership isn't a panacea for all that ails organizations and their relationships with their people. It's not a leadership philosophy for all precisely because it must align with leadership character to be effective, and character is individually manifested.

GROUNDED AND REALISTIC

Humility plays an important part in servancy and stewardship. The grounded and realistic leader goes beyond mere modesty. They also keep their, and others', feet planted firmly on the ground. They're diligent and hardworking. Servant leaders understand that great leaders aren't about grandiose plans and pronouncements about the bright future ahead. They don't puff themselves or others up with speeches that overlook the reality of the hard work that lies ahead. This doesn't mean that they don't use visions and motivation to drive performance. They just place these tools in perspective and balance them with a message about the practical efforts needed for success.

Servancy and stewardship is action-based. It includes reminding team members that *talking* about the great things to come is cheap and common. *Real* value comes from taking that first step, and the one after, to make gradual progress that evolves today into a better tomorrow. There's little glory in executing the details, and it's unlikely to capture your people's hearts or minds. Reminding the team that along with the exciting talk comes hard work keeps them grounded and manages their expectations of the journey. If they know it will be long, painful at times, and filled with pitfalls, they can steel themselves for the road ahead and avoid unexpected disappointment.

This is where planning, scheduling, and allocating resources comes in. Servant leaders keep people realistic about the efforts needed to turn dreams into reality—and like all good visions come to life, the details that must be executed to make it happen. Everyone must pay dues along the way that no one who enjoys real, enduring success can avoid. When you pay them, you earn the right to feel confident about your abilities because they are based on a genuine record of success.

The benefit of experience that you earn by doing and learning through mistakes helps you understand that knowledge is only a starting point in life. The smartest people in the room rarely succeed because of their raw intellect; they do so only when they apply it to good effect. That IQ score, the postgraduate degree, and the silver spoons of privilege rarely feed the hunger for true and sustained success. Hard, and at times painful, effort is what powers people toward achievement. We all serve others. That's the lesson new workforce entrants with shiny diplomas fail to grasp when they look for a shortcut up the ladder. Pay your dues; that's the only way "up."

Servant leaders remain grounded by understanding that their position doesn't exempt them from the hard and unglorious work we've just spoken of. Most of us have heard a leader somewhere say that "I wouldn't ask my people to do something I wouldn't do myself." Servancy leads with this in mind. Leaders engage themselves in hard work, right alongside their people, to help the group succeed.

There are several benefits of this simple act. The first is that your people see you as more credible. You aren't just making pronouncements and returning to the corner office—you're an active part of the solution by rolling your sleeves up to help. This increases your standing with the team as they see that you actually "know what you are talking about." When you take up occasional opportunities to personally integrate yourself into team activities, even for a short while, you demonstrate interest in your people and the work they do and evidence your commitment to their success. You also have the opportunity to listen to the voices of those nearest the customer.

James C. Hunter, in *The World's Most Powerful Leadership Principle*, stated that "humble leaders display a willingness, even an eagerness, to listen to the opinions of others and are wide open to contrary opinion. Humble leaders know they do not have to have all of the answers, and they are perfectly ok with that" (p. 95). When you are working alongside your people, why not listen carefully to the opinions of those serving the customer each day? At some point, they're bound to have better and more practical ideas than you've come up with. Harvesting that knowledge can be invaluable for the group's success. The team's full capacity of knowledge and expertise should be applied to the team's goals, after all.

The servant leader also knows that they need to have a sense of realism about the organization's resources, the capabilities of their people, and the vision that they create and communicate. Often, the egotist labels this as "thinking small" or a lack of ambition—which is unfortunate. Narcissism demands grandiosity; the "big" vision of tomorrow that outdoes those of others. The egotistical leader says, "I'm smarter than others, I'm better than others, and I therefore have a more accurate vision of tomorrow than them— so why shouldn't I think 'big' and inspire others to greatness?"

The problem with this perspective? It's out of touch with reality. There are very real limitations on the capacities of our people, the amount of time in a day, the emotional energy of team members, and the financial and other resources of the firm. Ludicrous goals that sound wonderful in theory and ridiculous in practice are initially captivating. They mesmerize people who aren't informed enough to discern delusion from ambition. Leaders who undertake such actions fool themselves and others and lead them down a path toward disillusion.

Those who may not think as "big" as the leader don't lack ambition and clarity of vision. They're willing to work just as hard to see a better tomorrow. But they also have seen disappointment, setbacks, and failures that lead them to believe the road ahead is filled with obstacles and adversities to overcome. Rather than accuse them of thinking small, listen to their words of caution and consider that they may just have valid viewpoints and wisdom to offer to the cause. What do you have to lose if they're wrong? And if they're right? Your own pride shouldn't keep you from success. Kouzes and Posner remind us that hubris is the greatest leadership sin of all, born out of the failure to remain grounded and modest (*A Leader's Legacy*, p. 158).

Grand ambition and a compelling, but wholly unrealistic, vision of tomorrow count for nothing in this world. Sycophants are easy to gather. The winners of any game develop strategies that they can successfully execute. The strategy may even be flawed, but that matters little compared to the person with the perfect plan who is unable to realize it. Big dreams come very, very cheap. We all have them. True ambition knows that to transform fantasy into reality, the bridge of realism has to be crossed—while others stand on the banks watching with their "big" ideas.

- *What do you do to help your people (and yourself) understand the level of hard work and dedication needed to achieve the group's aims?*
- *Do you "roll up your sleeves" to act as a resource, working alongside your team members to observe issues firsthand and help them succeed?*
- *Do you listen to the opinions of others who provide counsel and caution, or accuse them of "thinking small" when they voice concern about the "big plan" you've communicated?*
- *Before announcing ambitious plans, do you consider the resources available and chances of success, or do you "trust to hope" and your team's motivation?*

SELFLESS AND PROTECTING

Servant leaders focus first on their people, knowing that the business results they desire emanate from them. They focus on creating an environment where people can flourish—one that is safe and allows skills and experience to be actualized. Putting others before ourselves is the heart of servancy; it requires sacrifice, and that reality isn't suited to all those with ambition to lead. Ken Blanchard put it eloquently, stating that "the flock is not there for the sake of the shepherd; the shepherd is there for the sake of the flock" (*The Heart of a Leader*, p. 157).

The primary reason leaders exist is to serve the interests of their people. In doing so, they can also serve the organization's aims and its customers. These are not mutually exclusive concepts; they are mutually dependent. The difference occurs in where leaders start and where the satisfaction of the various stakeholders emanates from. Servancy advocates for the satisfaction of employee needs, believing that happy customers derive from happy employees. Those happy customers allow the organization to thrive and the leaders within it to achieve their professional aims.

If we focus first on others, we risk expending our own finite resources without any certain personal return. Others we support can still be ineffective and dissatisfied. We may be unable to close the loop that sees our sacrifices paid back to us with a dividend so that we, too, can gain in our own lives. There are no guarantees when you invest in people. Your sacrifices might come to nothing, it's true. All of this disappointment is a possibility, dependent upon how you define what your own success looks like.

Along with that risk, however, comes great opportunity. When group members' needs are satisfied, there's potential for greater productivity, engagement, innovation, customer satisfaction, and a culture of mutual supportiveness. All of these factors have the power to return to us and satisfy our own needs as they multiply. It's not just professional karma—it's great business. Servant leaders accept the risk that comes with the potential reward of multiplying their positive impact. They also understand how servancy can help them be better leaders as they support their teams.

When decisions are made with others' needs in mind, leaders take a more holistic, long-term view of situations that benefit their critical thinking and judgment. Personal pride becomes subordinate to supporting the team, so these leaders demonstrate flexibility rather than stubbornly sink further group time and effort into failing initiatives to avoid admitting their own mistakes. There's a calm conviction that comes with a focus on doing what is right for others.

If you're significantly driven to develop others, gravitate toward teamwork, look for mutual supportiveness in company cultures, and enjoy environments of inclusiveness and empowerment, then servant leadership may align well with your character and priorities. Because the reward often comes as a part of the journey of servant leadership, it can be particularly appealing. This doesn't mean that the servant leader has to make due only with the feeling of personal satisfaction. Adam Grant, in *Give and Take* (p. 74), also pointed out that in extensive research covering a wide range of industries, those who had an attitude of giving also earned more raises and promotions.

Demonstrating selflessness and a general attitude of servancy isn't complex; it just requires commitment to the mindset. Having provided vision and direction, your focus now shifts to being a resource for goal attainment. Ask your people what their questions and concerns are in trying to meet expectations. Find out what they need from you and from the organization. Help people overcome problems they encounter, and ease their journey by spotting obstacles and clearing the path.

Personally engage with your people, job shadowing to learn more about the issues they face in their daily work. Roll up your sleeves on occasion to work within the team where your position and skills make the biggest impact. Share the credit when success happens, and shoulder the blame when failures occur. Help your people navigate through the political realities of the organization to accelerate their progress. Introduce them to others who can also assist them in reaching goals, and build networks for team use.

It's not rocket science stuff here, but when you prove that your people matter to you more than your own interests, you begin to cement the health of your relationships with them. That means the foundations stick even when crises hit or you cause unintentional problems for the group. Your people will support you in kind and pull you out of the occasional hole that we all can dig for ourselves as leaders from time to time.

It's comforting when you know that your leader "has your back" and is watching out for your well-being. When leaders also demand that of team members, they build an environment that shelters people against the storms that can hit organizations. We are not alone. The safety that comes from numbers demonstrates our natural biological instinct: to move inward toward the center of the group when danger arises from outside. This flocking behavior happens commonly in the wild, and we've translated it to the work environment.

Simon Sinek aptly explains the role of leadership as protector in his wonderful read *Leaders Eat Last*. He stated, "by creating a Circle of Safety around the people in the organization, leadership reduces the threats people feel inside the group, which frees them up to focus more time and energy to protect the organization from the constant dangers outside and seize the big opportunities. Without a Circle of Safety people are forced to spend too much time and energy protecting themselves from each other" (p. 22).

This concept makes perfect sense. Have you ever had an emotionally unpredictable boss or one who created a constant feeling of uncertainty over your job security? Someone who eroded your confidence and self-esteem, refused to take counsel from others, and rarely allowed you to make meaningful decisions about your own work? Have you worked in an atmosphere dominated by office politics, intrigue, and a "me-first" attitude?

If you've ever experienced such an environment, you've likely spent a lot of time and emotional energy on self-preservation. When the work environment itself becomes the threat, we dread going to the office and focus our energy on just making it through the day with our jobs and sanity intact. This detracts significantly from our productivity and potential, and can also become a source of physical and emotional health issues in the long term. Most make the decision to move jobs in the end, taking their precious knowledge and experience with them.

Early in my career I worked with a leader who was very energetic, driven, and supportive. He knew my internal motivators and used them effectively for our mutual benefit. He was friendly, approachable, and a resource I could count on to help me learn from my mistakes. I also knew quite clearly that, if I repeatedly failed to produce expected results after all the support provided, I wouldn't have my job anymore. He'd do what he could to coach me up and provide help, but in the end he expected a payoff from his investment. I believed that was a very fair perspective, and I respected him for it. Along with the protection and support he provided came a price of entry and continued membership in the group: performance. He simply evidenced the expectations of any effective servant leader.

Another benefit of providing protection as servant leader is the free flow of information. Ken Blanchard, in *The Heart of a Leader*, said that "real communication happens when people feel safe" (p. 88). If you want to create an environment of innovation where others freely share ideas and opinions, you have to make it a safe place to do so. When others feel that their ideas can be expressed without recrimination, they'll share important details that allow for better decision-making and help the team avoid the occasional looming disaster.

Safety isn't to be confused with a lack of standards or ambition, however. Team members are never "safe" from the requirement to meet expectations around performance or behavior. Leaders set the tone within their teams by explaining the ground rules for entry and continued membership. They set expectations around how to share and debate ideas and opinions, how to resolve conflicts, and insist on personal accountability. Team members understand that threats to the group's well-being, productivity, and success shouldn't emanate from within the group itself. When violations of these expectations occur, the leader deals with them promptly and decisively. Group members witness that you're serious about preserving a culture of safety when you act on your commitment to it.

Take the occasional bullet for your team; you're the leader, after all. You have to accept responsibility for the work they do and the way they act, while holding them accountable for the same. When team members unintentionally make waves in the organization, help smooth the waters and protect them from the political minefields they may be stumbling into. You are there to help provide support for your people. Defend their interests when they have been mistreated by others, or misjudged based on inaccurate or incomplete information.

Make good-faith efforts to coach team members up before coaching out. Your staff will notice and blossom in an environment that feels more secure. As Michael Abrashoff stated in *It's Your Ship*, "leaders and managers need to understand that their employees are keenly attuned to their actions and reactions … If they see you intervene to help someone who is worth the effort, they will be reassured. Though the process is tedious and time consuming, you will benefit if people feel more secure, are more willing to take risks, and have a positive attitude about the organization" (p. 78).

- *Do you put the interests of your people before your own when making decisions?*
- *Do you regularly ask questions and listen in order to understand your team members' needs?*
- *Is your team a "safe" place where all understand the requirement to mutually support one another in order to remain a part of the team?*

EMOTIONAL SENSITIVITY AND NURTURING

Servancy and stewardship requires leaders to be attuned to others' strengths, weaknesses, fears, desires, and ambitions. You cannot serve well without knowing *how* to serve, and that's going to vary by individual. Just like motivation, servancy is individually experienced, and that requires a degree of emotional sensitivity. Consideration, tolerance, and empathy aren't the purview of everyone, however.

Stewardship requires the same. If you're entrusted with the care and nurturing of others before they move on to the next chapter in their careers, you need to know both *how* to best do so and *what* future ambitions you are developing toward. This can't be done through a detached, transactional form of leadership. It requires an understanding of others' feelings in order to work well. That required level of intimacy at work can be uncomfortable for some leaders to get past.

Like it or not, no one leaves their emotions at the door—encouraging our people to do so is an archaic style of leading. Today, we want people to come filled with emotion to work. Enthusiasm, ambition, empathy, compassion, contentment, and pride can all act as the fuel for workplace achievement and building cultures of greatness. An unfeeling boss can't tap into them. The environment the leader creates either ignites such emotions or smothers them.

We operationalize this as leaders by getting to know our people. When you interview and onboard staff, ask: What drives you to perform well in your job? What is the most creative and inspirational work environment you've been in, and why? What was the best supervisor you've ever worked with like? And the worst boss? What situations do you find most frustrating or difficult to cope with at work? What are your strongest workplace motivators? And demotivators? What are your career and life ambitions right now?

Most people will happily tell us about themselves if we just ask. Many leaders, however, feel uncomfortable getting to know their people in a more structured way. Instead, they prefer to hope that, by osmosis, they'll gain insight into their team members. Seize any opportunity to capture some time with your people individually; it offers a chance to gain some insight into them if you just make the effort and purposefully inquire.

When people have issues in or out of work, the occasional word of kindness and some emotional support never go amiss. How would you respond to problems and pain that a friend or relative is experiencing? Use that as the standard for how you should treat your work teammates. Some compassion and support—even in small doses—demonstrates that you're sensitive to delivering on the needs they have at work; needs that go beyond merely supporting their productivity.

Intimacy helps organizations combat dangers that always lurk. A "thumbs up or thumbs down" approach to quickly dealing with people issues such as hiring, promotions, and layoffs without careful contemplation for the lives affected is a callous way of determining the fate of those in an organization or those wishing to join it. It's not gladiatorial combat in ancient Rome. This is the modern workplace, and people deserve more consideration from their leaders than that. The layers of personnel that separate senior management from those who serve the customers also distance leaders from seeing the true effect of their actions on others. Leaders can become divorced from the consequences of their decisions and dehumanize their own workforce and the very patrons who are reason the business exists in the first place.

We can't forget that the decisions we may make in a rushed and glib manner for the sake of short-term results on the income statement have potential long-term effects on the lives of our team members and customers. This isn't idealism and naïve postulating. Ask any business that rushed to make such decisions for the sake of better near-term numbers to calculate the real long-term costs. Look at the organization's productivity, efficiency, reputation, continuity of service, knowledge base, customer retention, ability to hire and retain talent, and revenue and you will find that they often mortgaged the future at a price much higher than the smart people in the room imagined. No group should make such decisions without careful contemplation of the effects on all the stakeholders, not just the shareholders.

Long-term business sustainability can be cheaply bargained away. Likely, we've all witnessed or heard of an organization with an outstanding business model and a boatload of raw intellect at the top that can't attract and retain staff and deliver consistent excellence because management treats its people poorly. High IQs in the boardroom don't always translate well into EQs that result in effective relationship building, inspiration, motivation, and results. The most ingenious of business plans fail when the people who can actualize them aren't treated well and properly nurtured. Few would argue that treating people with care and consideration doesn't positively affect operational results.

While learning more about people's capabilities, aspirations, and fears, leaders also get to know their strengths, weaknesses, and drivers. This allows them to position their people better for maximum impact. Servancy also brings advantages with respect to how others come to feel about themselves, as Diana Whitney explains in *Appreciative Leadership*—"It also enables you to give the gift of *illumination* to others. By seeing, hearing, and describing strengths, you validate people, give them self-confidence, and offer up new and better ways for them to see themselves. You lay the foundation for or reinforce a stronger and more capable self-identity" (p. 69). It's always nice to be reminded of our unique value, to know that we have significance and that we matter to others. It's rocket fuel for the soul that lays the foundation for greater accomplishments.

Investments we make in others take time to show a return, if ever. Sometimes they come to nothing. Many leaders have a natural impatience for progress and results, which tempts them to use a directive approach. It's easier just to *tell* people what to do than to take the additional time develop and equip them to handle situations independently. It takes more effort to teach someone to fish than to just catch the fish for them. The latter technique allows you to quickly feed them today. They will, of course, come back to you again when they're hungry tomorrow. The former will help individuals feed themselves—and others—in the future.

People want to be nurtured so they can stand on their own two feet and use their capabilities more fully. They want to better realize their potential as human beings. Your ability to find out more about their capabilities and potential via your leadership approach will inform how to best nurture them for mutual benefit. This requires you to regularly check for barriers to growth that include both the working environment and your own approach to managing. It will also take some courage, humility, and frankness to have those productive discussions with your people.

- *Are you emotionally sensitive to the issues and problems your people experience, responding empathetically to them when the occasion calls for it?*
- *Do you regularly interact with your people (outside of work issues) so that you learn more about their interests and life ambitions?*
- *Do you nurture your people so that they learn to operate more independently in the future, or are you impatient and just provide them the answers instead?*

EMPOWERMENT AND INCLUSIVITY

You can't serve others without understanding that to *serve* is to be of use and to meet others' needs. This reality forces us to delegate power to others and allow them more control. This can be an uncomfortable place for leaders who prefer direct influence. The lack of control causes us stress, and guess what? Our people feel exactly the same way. Simon Sinek, in *Leaders Eat Last* (p. 29) references research that indicates the main cause of stress at work isn't the level of responsibility or pressure that comes when we progress up the ladder—it's the lack of control we feel we have over our work.

This shouldn't surprise anyone. There's little wonder that much of the angst we feel occurs when we have responsibility without authority. A sense of pride and managerial inertia causes us to grip our power tightly once we've obtained it as leaders. We've earned it, after all. That's why we were placed in the position in the first place, isn't it? To make decisions, "make things happen," and exercise as much personal control over outcomes as we can.

Traditional management beliefs hold that we're placed in the position to direct those less knowledgeable and capable of captaining their own fate. It's out of keeping with the way most people want to be led, however, as they work toward self-actualization in their own lives. The leader's role is *to obtain results via others' work*. It doesn't mean we always need to steer the ship to do so. A ship's captain doesn't personally steer the ship twenty-four hours a day out at sea. Others are empowered to do so capably while the captain rests or attends to other duties.

> Leaders should never get hung up with being "in charge." They should always keep their focus on the destination. They should be asking themselves, where are we going and how are we planning to get there? Who's the best person at this moment to lead the process of getting us from where we are to where we want to be? Is it me? Or is it another member of our team? Where does the expertise lie? Who's best connected to the sources of information? Who's got the most creative and innovative ideas that'll help us all succeed? (Kouzes and Posner, *A Leader's Legacy,* p. 125)

There are plenty of instances in which the most capable person to lead a discussion or initiative isn't you. In fact, that's why you hire experts into positions and develop people's capabilities to gain that expertise. The alternative is for you to take on more of the burden yourself as the workload and scope of responsibility increases. While we all may start our careers as very active "hands-on" leaders with task responsibilities ourselves, as our leadership and the business evolves we reach a crossroads. We can choose to keep doing the work ourselves as the volume grows, attempting to maintain more personal control. The risk, of course, is career burnout and a transition toward more tactical work because of our lack of delegation.

When you delegate responsibility to others, several important benefits occur. The most obvious is that you can get some sleep at night because you've just increased the resource base available to you. You spread the burden, matching expertise to initiatives in a way that increases the chances of success far beyond that which you could have accomplished on your own. After all, you're not an expert at *everything*, as much as your pride might tell you otherwise.

Think about the initiatives and deliverables your team is responsible for. What are the underlying tasks and behaviors? Which have you assigned to yourself and which to others on your team? Can you delegate more of your tasks to others, allowing them to take on more responsibility and authority without overwhelming them? Leaders commonly rationalize their reluctance to give away power on the current workload of their people without really talking to them or exploring how work can be reprioritized, redistributed, or tasks ended altogether that are no longer relevant.

Opportunities always exist to delegate some of the more tactical work to your people, allowing them to expand their skills and experience as well as provide them more responsibility and autonomy. This frees you up to deal with the tasks better suited to your own position level, skills, and experience. Manage by objective, not by dictating how to do the work down to the last detail. In doing so, you'll find you've built a more flexible, capable workforce along the way.

Ask your team members to report progress on the delegated tasks in group settings. This keeps everyone informed about the work individuals are responsible for, allows for idea-sharing, and builds accountability for results. Allow people to own the problems and mistakes they encounter, asking them questions in a helpful manner regarding how they're addressing issues. This guides them toward solutions rather than tells them "the way you'd do it." If staff are always beholden to working exactly how and when you'd do it, then you don't really need their hearts or minds. People only stay in such work environments until something better comes along—and it always does.

Exclusivity strangles innovation and others' willingness to provide input. It also risks the quality of decision-making because you fail to acknowledge the value of others' thinking. Bill George described this danger, stating, "leaders who lead only with their intellect tend to dismiss the opinions of others and dominate decision making. As a result, they overpower less forceful voices that have vital ideas, insights, and answers needed for sound decision making. Leaders with exceptionally high IQs often get too intellectually involved and may be intolerant of others with less raw intellect" (*Discover Your True North*, p. 84).

As leaders when we invite people into the process of idea-sharing and decisioning, we signal that they matter. We gain the benefit of more information and differing perspectives in decisioning and creating best practice. We ensure that important details aren't left unearthed because of our own blind spots. We also gain greater commitment from those who were involved in the dialogue, whether or not their opinions won the day.

Often, the best ideas come from those actively engaged in the work and closest to the customer. Your role isn't to dominate the process of idea generation but to create an environment where ideas come to light and are given due consideration, whatever the source. Your role is to listen. If true and empathetic listening occurs, you can then generate good questions. Questions that are relevant, aid in consideration of alternatives, and help resolve problems are like nuggets of gold.

Inclusivity requires transparency and free flow of information up and down the hierarchy. Staff need information about the issues that affect them and their positions. When you withhold that information, you're indicating that you neither trust them nor view them as significant enough to include them in communication. This obviously doesn't engender feelings of positivity, loyalty, or support. Staff also can't help resolve issues if they aren't included in the conversation. Information empowers your people to make responsible decisions to help the organization be successful. This sense of responsibility is referenced in Kouzes and Posner's *A Leader's Legacy* (p. 86), in which they quite rightly point out that personal responsibility can't exist independent of free choice. And people crave freedom.

Talk about issues openly with the group whenever you can and use scheduled team meetings for this purpose. Ask for opinions and help. Speak individually with team members you believe may have particular expertise to provide. Discuss what concerns team members have with alternative courses of action.

As leaders, we all know that we can't involve our people in every single decision that affects them, and some decisions impact your people that you don't personally make. We're all responsible to someone, and decisions in the boardroom or elsewhere will change our people's work experiences. That doesn't keep you from inclusive decision-making on those matters that *do* arise from your leadership, however. It also doesn't prevent you from talking through questions or concerns on decisions already made elsewhere so everyone can acknowledge the reality of the situation and move forward constructively.

Neither work nor life in general runs via pure democracy, but how we approach inclusiveness affects our people's engagement and efforts to see decisions through. If an important aspect of our role is also to expand the pool of potential leaders, we need to include others in dialogue and provide them the opportunities that hone critical thinking and decisioning skills. Along the way, we also tap into their potential to propel the organization forward.

—————————————→

- *Do you regularly include your people in conversations about issues that affect them and decisions that may impact the success of the team?*
- *Are others empowered to use their discretion and make decisions about their work, including those that affect the customer?*
- *Are empowered team members held accountable for providing progress updates and for the outcomes of their decision-making?*

←—————————————

AUTHENTICITY

Many of us spend much of our careers trying to find our own voice and forge a style of leadership true to our values, beliefs, and personality. Like anyone else, we model behavior from current and prior supervisors and from observation and mentors. We scour books, consume TED Talks and other online media, and attend seminars to hone our leadership skills. In doing so, we may try to "be" like those other leaders we admire rather than just integrating aspects of their leadership into our own.

We're tempted to suppress our dissenting opinions just to fit in with the group, or model less admirable behavior to conform rather than be a force for change. Although one of life's ironies is that we spend our youth trying to fit in and our adult life trying to stand out, we also know that the tall blade of grass is the one first cut down. So at times, conforming feels like the safe choice.

No "one size fits all" leadership approach exists, which I'm sure you know already. There are only others' practices and perspectives that you may consider as you chart your own leadership path. Indeed, this very book discusses some competencies which, in my opinion, are core to effective leadership. You may have a different opinion, and that's quite okay. That very debate adds richness to the narrative on leadership and helps each of us discover our leadership destiny.

You've got to be humble enough to admit that you're always on the journey in leadership and will never arrive at the destination. You're always learning about yourself, always refining your skills, and always applying your expertise to a new situation. Authentic leadership requires us to abandon facades, which include portrayals of infallibility. Your people *already know* you make mistakes, have flaws, can't do it all on your own, and aren't all-knowing. Your ability to acknowledge these realities openly strengthens the bond with your people, not weakens it. Your team members' respect for you grows, and if well-treated, they will support you, cover for your weaknesses, and save you from yourself occasionally.

Bill George, in *Finding Your True North*, acknowledged this in his own leadership, stating that "over many years of my career, I felt I had to do things perfectly and have all the answers. I lacked the confidence to share my weaknesses, fears, and vulnerabilities. When I finally learned to do so, things went much better for me, and my relationships with colleagues improved. Most important, I felt more comfortable in my skin and had a stronger sense of well-being" (p. 89).

When you share your own stories—including your flaws, fears, desires, and motivations—you signal that you'd like others to do the same. You show others that it's okay to be vulnerable, make mistakes, and ask for help because you've just told them that you experience these things too. We seek honest and open communication from our people so that we can gather the information to help them resolve issues and support success. That's exactly what others also seek from us.

If you've ever been in an environment where a very minor personal infraction or dissenting opinion leads to blistering condemnation from the boss, you know exactly what to do—you simply stop sharing of yourself. You decide not to be the tall blade of grass. When the boss who says they don't want "yes" men around them really does, sharing your perspective and expertise makes no difference. Self-preservation becomes the order of the day, and your time and talent are squandered in the workplace. Frustrated, intolerant geniuses are left to climb the mountain alone, succeed much less often, and take much longer if they do eventually reach the top.

It's a pity, really. Our people deserve more humanity from leadership than that. When we share stories of our own mistakes and what we learned from them, we open others to the possibility that sharing the same won't lead to negative repercussions. People withhold themselves less often. Rather than cover up mistakes or try to handle problems themselves to avoid fallout, they're forthcoming so we can help them navigate through rough waters successfully.

I've always said to my team that unpleasant surprises are what I like to avoid most, so if problems arise or mistakes are made, let me know so that I can help while there's still time to make a difference. When someone makes a mistake and you help them resolve the issue and learn along the way, others will see you as part of the solution rather than part of the problem. They will come to you again when they have to rely on your help, rather than gifting you with that unpleasant surprise. This doesn't mean we don't hold people accountable for minimizing large errors or repeated mistakes. Our focus is still on quality and performance, but when fear and avoiding pain is the motivator for our people, they learn little about how to deal with similar problems in future.

As I write this, the world is engulfed in one of the largest health crises in a century in 2020 and 2021. Lifestyles and work processes have been significantly altered, and we've found that people in T-shirts and pajamas at home can do perfectly good work in front of their computers. When videoconferences occur, they can dress and present professionally without the benefit of cufflinks and ties. Content wins out over form in the end, as it should. If you're communicating in a stiff, dispassionate manner primarily to keep up appearances and impress yourself, stop. Your people are unlikely to find it an endearing quality that builds rapport. They'd prefer a professional—but above all genuine—version of you that they can understand more easily and relate to.

- *Do you display your "true" self to your people or put on a facade and try to act out your leadership in a disingenuous way?*
- *Do you authentically share stories of your own flaws, mistakes, and vulnerabilities, and are you open and honest in your communication?*
- *Do you communicate in a warm, authentic way that strikes a good balance between professionalism and the informality that helps build rapport?*

PROVIDING PURPOSE AND SIGNIFICANCE

Servant leaders assume the role of *visionary*, making purpose and meaning work for their people. When we have a purpose that goes beyond ourselves, motivation is enhanced because others depend on and benefit from us. The "what does it all mean?" question is answered in a way that puts our day in the context of the larger story of our lives. If our reason for getting up while it is still dark out and fighting traffic into work is only "the paycheck," how long is that going to inspire us to keep repeating the process?

While the paycheck helps you fulfill obligations to your family's financial security, over time a sense of emptiness wells up where significance should instead reside. You feel like Sisyphus, rolling the immense boulder up the hill each day only to watch it roll back down again so you can repeat the process. None of this inspires continued and full engagement in your own life.

You can change your circumstances, including the job you do and who you do it for. There's risk associated with such a change, but, of course, reward potential also exists. Will the change in coworkers, boss, organizational culture and structure, systems, procedures, products/services, and customers lead to the more fulfilling work experience you'd hoped for? It all might just pay off handsomely.

There's another option though. You can change your perspective on your current circumstances in order to take more meaning from them today. Mark Sanborn's excellent book *The Fred Factor* describes how his local postman's creative view on how to add value to his customers' lives led him to greater job fulfillment. He took what may seem like a mundane activity—delivering the mail—and delivered extraordinary service along the way. An "ordinary" task completed with extraordinary care and creativity led to a fulfilling career for Fred and an excellent experience for all those whose lives he touched. "Purpose is the context that frames all of our life experiences into a meaningful whole. If we have it, all the challenging experiences of life serve to forge our identity and character. Although life may be challenging, every experience is our teacher, and every challenge an opportunity to live more purposefully" (Kevin Cashman, *Leadership from the Inside Out*, pp. 67-68).

Many leaders, in the process of acquiring talent, onboarding staff, and training and coaching for performance, get caught up in ensuring the procedural competence of their people without really acknowledging that the hands and feet go where the heart and head tell them to. Remember that excellence is where passion and talent collide. Purpose takes that concept a layer deeper because it is purpose that precedes the development of passion. It answers the question of "Why should I be passionate?" in the first place. If we're to develop excellence in our team members, we have to forge purpose to ignite passion and develop talent to see that passion fulfilled.

If you don't believe you've got the personal charisma to pull off such interactions with your staff, don't worry. We're not talking about rousing, dramatic speeches here. As a leader, you can weave some practical tasks into your work to help provide significance to others' work lives. The first happens *before* they even come to work for you: When you engage with job candidates, do you talk about the company's mission and your team's purpose? Do you discuss the purpose of their potential role and how it impacts the team, organization, and customers? Do you ask candidates what they're passionate about? You want people who can identify with your *purpose* before you make the decision to hire.

Imbue your people with purpose during the onboarding phase of their employment as well. Orientation meetings often serve the purpose of discussing the organization's mission and impact on those they serve. Individual discussions with your new hire help outline how the role influences the work and results of others on the team and how their performance will impact the organization and customers. There's also great value in providing customer and employee testimonials to provide purpose and significance to work. You reinforce this when new team members carry out their duties successfully and positive impacts are discussed with them so they can "see and feel" how their work adds value to others.

When noteworthy contributions and successes occur within the team and organization, share them. People vicariously interpret meaning for their roles via others' achievements. In an increasingly interdependent working world, few people's success is their province alone. Typically, achievements are due to some element of teamwork. Talk about successes in group meetings, one-on-ones, annual appraisals, intranet, email, and corporate newsletters. People need periodic reminding of "why we do this" in order to be fully engaged and retained.

People don't identify with business in the aggregate. As individuals, we identify with stories of impact on *individuals*. When we hear of the positive difference our work has made to others' lives, passionately relayed by customers firsthand, we can't help but become more invested in our jobs. We're no longer in the business of mortgage lending, manufacturing, or retail sales—we're in the "making a difference in people's lives business." In the long term, those ties bind us to our roles and the company much more than our paychecks or other tangible rewards. As leaders, when we help others find their own unique path to meaning we serve everyone well because we provide greater opportunity for passion and talent to collide.

- *Do you help your people discover meaning and significance in their work by communicating purpose in a way that connects with their interests and values?*

- *Do you use individual employees' and customers' testimonials to provide evidence of how people's work impacts "a greater good" that goes beyond just making the company money?*
- *Do you discuss purpose, meaning, and significance consistently, from recruiting and onboarding to ongoing training, communication, and appraisal activities?*

APPRECIATION AND ENCOURAGEMENT

Appreciation should occur when the "right" behaviors lead to positive customer impacts and successful goal attainment. It may also occur for reasons other than performance that reflect the value people bring to the team for *who they are* not just *what they do*. Encouragement helps us all along the journey, particularly when we encounter obstacles or the race feels emotionally draining. Preeminent leadership author and consultant John Maxwell echoed these sentiments in his book *Encouragement Changes Everything*, stating, "when we're on the brink of failure, the right words at the right time can keep us in the game. When we're too tired or discouraged to keep going, an act of compassion can give us new strength. There's no doubt about it: Encouragement enables us to persevere like nothing else" (p. 15). Appreciation and encouragement act as the mortar to a healthy relationship foundation with your people.

Whereas recognition normally occurs after the fact to acknowledge results, appreciation and encouragement are often anticipatory. We provide them prior to task completion to propel others to fulfill more of their potential and increase performance. They enhance self-esteem and confidence.

The *Pygmalion Effect* evidences these forces at work. If you're a parent who's had a child about to participate in a sporting event, music recital, or some other endeavor, what do you normally say? "You're going to do great!" Now if we're honest, we don't know how our child is going to perform, but we utter those words to encourage our child, signal our love and support, and enhance the self-confidence of our little one so that they put in their best effort. That's all we really hope for. Guess what? That very same concept works for adults too.

The Pygmalion Effect has been studied in a wide variety of environments, from the military to educational settings. When compared to control groups offered no appreciation for their potential, or encouragement, people who were provided appreciation and encouragement in advance *actually performed measurably better* in future than their counterparts. In other words, emotional intelligence applied at the right time positively affects future performance. It causes others to prove, to a greater degree, that our expressed appreciation and confidence in them was well-placed. It's nice to be around encouraging, appreciative people. We like to repay their compliments through our results and hopefully earn more appreciation and encouragement along the way.

To positively impact performance and improve your relationships, the message is a simple one: Take the time and effort to provide appreciation and encouragement. If you stop to consider it, there's something to appreciate in everyone. Build this into your individual meetings. Express gratitude in group settings for who your people are—not just for their accomplishments. When tough situations arise and your team encounters obstacles, encourage your people and show belief in their potential to overcome adversity. When you see improvement on the way toward reaching expectations, supply some fuel for the journey through a few well-chosen words.

If you want to get more out of your people then help them see both how far they've already come and their ability to fulfill more of their potential. It works. In Adam Grant's great book *Give and Take* (pp. 100-101) the work of researcher Brian McNatt is referenced. McNatt conducted a meta-analysis of seventeen studies covering thousands of subjects. He concluded that when managers view employees as "bloomers," employees subsequently blossomed in their roles. McNatt found that managers' perspectives about their staff meaningfully affects their future performance, and he encouraged leaders to understand the power that genuine interest in, and belief in the potential of, their staff has.

Appreciation and encouragement cost you exactly nothing. It's an absolutely free manner of engaging, retaining, and enhancing people's performance. It relies only on your interest and emotional intelligence in engaging them. It requires personal leadership involvement, which isn't something all leaders are prepared to do despite the payoff potential.

The vast majority of leaders want encouragement themselves and acknowledge its positive role in the workplace. The unfortunate irony is that, despite this reality, leaders appear reluctant to provide others what they so desperately crave themselves. Chapman and White, in *The Five Languages of Appreciation in the Workplace*, state that "the greatest tragedy we have observed is that while most managers, supervisors, and colleagues genuinely appreciate the people with whom they work, they often neglect to verbally express that appreciation" (p. 58).

So why do leaders resist providing for others what they wish for themselves? The answer lies in more traditionalist views about recognition, reward, appreciation, and encouragement. Older perspectives see these items as precious commodities to be carefully rationed in order to support their exchange rate. The belief is that when we "flood the market" with appreciation and encouragement, their value decreases and so buys less goodwill and discretionary effort with each act. To prop up the value of appreciation and encouragement, we need to control the supply to create enough demand to maximize effort.

This logic is outdated and it seems clear that, based on research and employee feedback, most team members don't believe a proper balance has been struck because they continue to crave more appreciation. It's counterintuitive for leaders to deny their own people the emotional resources that they themselves demand more of in order to invest themselves in their work. Think about each of your team members. If you can't remember the last time you expressed your appreciation and encouraged them, then perhaps it's time to rethink how you're using these free resources.

- *Do you consciously build in opportunities to express appreciation and encouragement for your people, both in individual and group meetings?*
- *When did you last express appreciation, encouragement, or recognition to each of the individuals on your team?*
- *Do you appreciate, encourage, and recognize your people as soon as you identify the opportunity to use these resources?*

Section 6

MANAGING CHANGE

T he only constant in life is change. In today's business environment, that's certainly true. The VUCA (volatile, uncertain, complex, ambiguous) world we live in seems to be getting more "VUCA" each day. I certainly didn't think, only a year ago, that I'd be writing this in the midst of the COVID-19 crisis, one of the worst health pandemics of the last century, which has caused a global economic meltdown and greatly affected how we work, live, and travel. As much as we'd like to think that, in business or in life, we can control the winds or even harness them in a predictable way, in many cases that just isn't reality.

Unanticipated forces cause organizations to react through change, and planned business transformations also mean the implementation of change initiatives. On a smaller scale, change happens within business units, functions, or teams that at least alters a part of how we work and who we work with. Change is now the "new normal," with periods of calm and stability occasionally happening in between.

Change might cause an uneasy feeling to creep into the pit of our stomachs—that feeling of disorientation, where we long for something concrete to stand on rather than the continually the shifting sand beneath our feet. The comfort of knowing that tomorrow will look the same as today, which is important for some, no longer exists. It's been replaced with the reality that whatever we know, whatever we do, and whatever we're "good at" today will become obsolete in the future and we'll have to reinvent ourselves yet again. It's no wonder workplace stress, absenteeism, disengagement, and productivity issues are regular challenges.

Along with change comes opportunity, however. The risks to people and organizations are real, but so are the potential rewards. Change offers opportunity and challenge, and transforming ourselves can energize and excite us. The learning and experience that accompanies change may also be very valuable. Renewal has great appeal, and organizations that negotiate change effectively and outmaneuver the competition thrive while others fight just to survive.

The ever-increasing pace and frequency of change affects the way organizations structure their operations today. Hierarchical structures and centralized decision-making are less common, as distance between the corner office and the end consumer slows down change progress. Authority and discretion are pushed out to the most local level practical to speed up decisioning and ensure the ability of the organization to be nimble.

Change initiatives involve people and process. This demands both *management* and *leadership* skills. Normally associated with analysis, planning, scheduling, resource allocation, and budgeting, *management* is an important component supporting process-based activities related to change. *Leadership*, by contrast, is focused on issues such as creating vision, motivation, collaboration, conflict management, and emotional support. These are the people-based activities that are also critical for change success.

Organizations are, of course, made up of people and it's people who drive, resist, embrace, react to, implement, communicate, monitor, and succeed or fail at change. With ever-increasing pace and overall levels of change, an air of cynicism can pervade the work environment. More change initiatives mean more opportunity for people to witness leadership incompetence in executing them. That, together with the natural human bias toward negativity that continual improvement initiatives unwittingly contribute to (the skeptic would say "It's never good enough"), means that change resistance is a regular by-product of dynamic work environments.

With a number of negative effects of poor change execution—including lower adoption rates of "the new way," failure of adoption altogether, slow pace of adaptation, decreased productivity, morale and turnover issues, customer complaints and loss, increased workplace stress, and absenteeism—it's clear that poor change management results in a heavy erosion of change benefits.

Despite the crucial need to address the people issues if change is to be successful, Julie Hodges, in her insightful book *Managing and Leading People through Organizational Change* (p. 3), references Woodward and Hendry's research indicating that one-third of senior managers admit that the people aspects of change initiatives are regularly ignored. It's simply easier to define and implement solutions focused on process rather than manage intangibles such as motivation and emotion, which also complicate matters because they're individually-based.

Change is undeniably both emotional and procedural. People are creatures of emotion; it's what drives our thoughts and behaviors. "As Robert French so eloquently says, 'merely to alter the arrangement of the furniture in a room or to appoint just one new member of staff can be enough to set the cats of anxiety and selfishness amongst the pigeons of stability and cooperation' " (Hodges, *Managing and Leading People through Organizational Change*, p. 50). The people-side of change is *transition*, which happens differently and at different paces for each person (and also at a different pace to change itself).

You can't neatly "process map" your people's emotional journey through change because no one experiences it in exactly the same way. This is the challenge for us. Leaders have to adapt to each team member's needs based on their unique transition path. That's the reality of change that challenges our leadership skills most.

You may have the resources, a well-detailed plan, and a "right" solution, but that doesn't guarantee that people will embrace it or use it consistently. Some people will work around the change, covertly trying to maintain the status quo or do it their own way. Others will use the "new way" effectively, and some will struggle to become competent. Certain team members will quickly make the transition while others will fail to do so altogether. All of this hinges on the talents and emotions of individuals in the team. "Bad" past change experiences with you and the organization breed cynicism and contempt, while "good" ones produce a better emotional foundation for change.

In many cases, people will work in their own self-interest, not just in times of change. We do, after all, what benefits us in most cases. Truly selfless acts are rare, as noble as they may be. As a leader you know that when you ask any of your staff to do something (including making changes), you need to answer the "what's in it for me" question for them. The same change affecting people in the same position on the same team can yet provide different benefits (or obstacles) to each, and you have to address those individual realities sooner or later—and sooner is better.

Being a leader isn't easy, particularly during times of change, but it can be exciting. You not only have the challenge of navigating your team members through change but also have to manage your own transition. Your emotions during change color your perspective on it, from which you think and act in your role. To constructively navigate others through change you first have to be in a healthy emotional place to cope with change yourself. You must motivate others to join the change journey even while you may not completely agree with the change. Just as team members individually experience change, it's also individually led by managers—each with their own unique set of talents, feelings, and views about the situation. This makes controlling the path and outcomes of change even more precarious for organizations.

Few leaders agree with the what, how, or why of change completely, and despite that reality, they're still responsible for ensuring that change initiatives are effectively managed. No leader has the luxury of simply opting themselves and their teams out of change simply because they don't like the timing or the way it's being implemented elsewhere in the organization. Every leader has the responsibility of making change initiatives as successful as possible within their own teams.

CREATING AWARENESS AND
URGENCY AROUND CHANGE

While change may certainly bring improvement, opportunities, excitement, variety, and "a better tomorrow," it also can present stress, uncertainty, fear, confusion, pain, and loss to people. Being in transition takes up people's finite emotional energy, time, and attention. In a world where more change happens—and more quickly—we guard ourselves against involvement in change that we believe is unnecessary. Because of the risk that accompanies change, it's natural to avoid it unless it's imperative or the benefits are clear. As a leader, this means you need to state a persuasive case for change.

On one hand, change can be reactive, driven by the external environment and forcing the organization to respond. Other changes are driven from within; they don't arise from crisis, but instead from opportunity or positioning for growth. Whatever the circumstance, to shift hearts, minds, hands, and feet to where you want them to be tomorrow you need to create a sense of urgency for change among your people:

> ... whether the starting point is good performance or bad, in the more successful cases I have witnessed, an individual or a group always facilitates a frank discussion of potentially unpleasant facts about new competition, shrinking margins, decreasing market share, flat earnings, lack of revenue growth, or other relevant indices of a declining competitive position ... The purpose of all this activity, in the words of one former CEO of a large European company, is "to make the status quo seem more dangerous than launching into the unknown." (John Kotter, from the article "Leading Change" in Harvard Business Review Press' *On Change Management*, p. 6)

The facts can often speak convincingly for themselves. Industry and company performance trends, financial results, customer complaint and retention data, per-employee efficiency/revenue/profit data, and team KPIs can all point to necessary change. If you can represent this information graphically, it's even better. Lay the foundation for change with data, logic, and a rational approach. Try to capture the mind at this stage, remembering that how we think triggers how we feel.

The facts may lead people to conclude that suffering is coming and that the pain of inaction will outweigh the trials caused by change. Let the team's minds wander down dark corridors, finding unpleasant conclusions behind every door. Some fear and anxiety are constructive at this point, as we know that basic human instincts are to seek pleasure and avoid pain. In this case it's about moving away from pain.

You can even pre-empt the conversation by placing your people in a position to personally experience the pain and discomfort you want to move away from. For instance: 1) Make your people try to complete tasks using an obsolete or broken process, 2) Have individuals periodically audit procedures to confirm that they've become irrelevant and ineffective, 3) Require staff and managers to personally interact with complaining customers.

Frustration, embarrassment, helplessness, and triviality can all cause people to truly internalize the need for change. Heath and Heath, in their wonderful book on change *Switch*, say that "trying to fight inertia and indifference with analytical arguments is like tossing a fire extinguisher to someone who's drowning. The solution doesn't match the problem" (p. 107). You want to evoke emotions, even though they are negative. Logic alone won't cause action. Make people feel the pain of today's reality, and they'll want to move away from it as long as the long-term benefits stack up well against the short-term costs.

If the change you're seeking isn't a response to crisis or current problems, then avoiding pain doesn't really exist as an influencing tool. If change is part of incremental improvement, an attempt to seize opportunity for growth, or proactive innovation, then the focus is about moving toward a "new and improved" state instead. The status quo may work but simply "isn't as good" as the future you're envisioning.

While the challenge of selling change may seem larger in this case, it shouldn't distract from using a similar approach focused first on hearts and minds. The facts you present may be about industry trends, customer preferences, new technology, and innovative processes. Supported by information about the benefits realized by other organizations that implemented change, people can connect the dots between success elsewhere and an improved, healthier future in their current organization. Spell it out for your people in clear and simple terms so that they understand how you've determined the benefits of change.

At this point, your people need to know that you're just beginning a dialogue to identify the need for change and that you don't have all the answers or a planned course of action yet. You're just "working the room" initially to identify who's in favor of exploring change and who is more skeptical. You can then tailor future messages so that you have a greater chance of growing advocacy for change. The less time and effort you spend now on this step, the more resistance you're going to encounter as you move further down the change path.

Leaders must acknowledge that a fundamental difference exists between awareness and desire for change. For instance, if I told you that smoking was bad for you, as is drinking too much alcohol or eating food high in saturated fats, you might know this already—and may have known for quite a long time. But moving from knowing to action are two very different things. A lack of action comes from the way we think about an issue, as the way we think becomes the way we feel—and the way we feel motivates behavior.

Get people to think differently and you'll make progress in getting them to take that first step toward change. For many this first step is having an open mind to the possibility that change is an appropriate course of action, and also a willingness to keep listening and constructively participating as the process unfolds.

⸻⸻⸻⟶

- *Do you come to discussions with your staff with facts, data, and logic to create a sense of urgency for change on your team?*
- *Do you take opportunities to have your people directly experience the issues and "broken" processes of today so they can understand why change is needed?*
- *Do you consider how the information you present will evoke an emotional reaction in your people so that you can create a sense of urgency for change within them?*

⟵⸻⸻⸻

DISCUSS THE CONSIDERATIONS INVOLVED IN MAKING THE CHANGE

Next, engage in conversation about the considerations involved in making change happen. Your people are going to provide valuable feedback on the change you're contemplating. Enter with an open mind, and be as objective as you can. Don't defend the change; just ask questions and listen. By arguing, you shut down the dialogue instead of learning from your people, which is the whole point of the exercise. If you stifle dialogue, you'll make change more difficult because people will believe that either you don't understand them, or worse—that you don't care about their thoughts and feelings.

Even if you think you understand the problem or opportunity fueling change, you almost certainly have an incomplete picture of it. The information your people bring to the table helps you have a more complete view. Before you begin to think about potential solutions you need to know the problem well, and there's no better source of input than the people who are experiencing it through their work with end customers. When you exclude people from the process it signals that you don't believe what they have to say has merit, and their reaction is bound to be resistance.

If your change situation is based on capturing opportunity, this dialogue with your team is no less important. Identifying and defining the opportunity will generate better change solutions. Perhaps additional opportunities will arise as a result of the discussion that reframes future thinking around business priorities. Dialogue will also help you gauge the passion—or indifference—individuals have for the opportunity and how challenging it will be to engage them in it.

Whether change involves problem resolution, crisis response, innovation, or capturing opportunity, dialogue helps skeptics move toward acceptance via their involvement in the process of coauthoring better solutions. It also brings the unconditional advocate back down to earth, helping them comprehend the issues and obstacles to be faced along the change journey. This helps them avoid future disappointment when success isn't nearly as easy to come by as they first thought. By bringing the extremes of people's viewpoints, either positive or negative, back toward the center the team becomes better grounded to face the realities of change that lie ahead of them.

Change never happens in a vacuum. This is where your people's input is critical, as they understand the implications of change on daily tasks and behaviors in a way in which you aren't fully aware. Although a change solution hasn't been settled on yet, it's useful to discuss the general knock-on effects that the primary change is likely to trigger. The discussion will turn toward more specific effects once a solution path has been chosen, but there are going to be some common secondary changes to identify at this point.

Assuming that *a* change is made—not yet identifying exactly *what* it is or *how* it will be accomplished—talking through employee concerns is important to help you choose the right solution. For instance, what secondary changes to workflow and process *might* you need to consider? Is the change going to complicate workflow and process or make it simpler? Will you need to create new procedures or alter existing ones? Will the change require the team to adopt new technology or alter existing systems? Understanding that a change initiative will likely involve small changes related to systems, processes, training and development, team structure, workflow, and communication, it's important to come up with a good plan. Don't overwhelm any of the participants with discussion about every detail at this point; just outline some of the major change considerations.

Let the group know that you're interested in their input so that you can better determine how to proceed. They'll appreciate your willingness to listen to them. People are likely to come up with issues that you hadn't considered, which will help you create a better plan once you've settled on a change solution. Let your team members uncover the minefields you may encounter so you don't stumble into them blindly.

If you want to increase the chances of a quality change solution and team support for it, involve your people in the process as much as is practical. Julie Hodges also advocates this perspective in *Managing and Leading People through Organizational Change,* stating: "People often say that they do not know how they fit into the change because they have not been involved in the planning process. The response from managers tends to be: 'Here's the change; this is why we have to change, here's how it will change—now own the change.' This does not work. What does work is ownership … Ownership is often best created by involving people in identifying problems and crafting solutions" (pp. 158-159).

- *Do you listen to your people regarding the issues and considerations involved with making the change you are considering?*
- *Do you consider your people's ideas and their suggestions regarding the additional expertise and resources needed to implement the change successfully?*
- *Do you understand the value of these discussions in helping people feel valued and included, which helps build greater support for change?*

COMMUNICATE THE CHANGE VISION

The next step? Create and communicate the change vision based on the "better tomorrow" you desire. Now is the time to craft a picture for your people of what the "new and improved" future looks like when change has been successfully implemented. Previously, we've talked about how having a manager with vision is one of the primary motivators in the workplace, and this is really no different. It's simply about casting vision around one specific area—change—to drive your people to the destination you want.

To increase the chances of success, consider some of the vision characteristics that are most impactful. The first is that it has to be appealing. Where *vision benefits > status quo + pain of transition* then you have much greater potential to win hearts and minds. Make the picture vivid in people's minds so that they can see and feel that "better tomorrow." Use analogies and stories so that they can relate to the vision and it becomes rich in their minds.

People won't follow what they can't understand—that's called blind faith, and it's in extremely short supply these days. Complex visions are hard to explain and communicate, and they inevitably breed mistrust. People's natural inclination today is to treat management with healthy skepticism, and when they think the boss is trying to dazzle them with nonsense and jargon they feel that they're being manipulated. Reduce that feeling by laying out your vision in clear and simple terms. This is your "elevator speech on change," and by the time it reaches the top floor you need to be done with the sales pitch to your team.

Business, leadership and change expert John Kotter said in *Leading Change* that "the time and energy required for effective vision communication are directly related to the clarity and simplicity of the message. Focused, jargon-free information can be disseminated to large groups of people at a fraction of the cost of clumsy, complicated communication. Technobabble and MBA-speak just get in the way, creating confusion, suspicion, and alienation. Communication seems to work best when it is so direct and so simple that it has a sort of elegance" (p. 89). Follow that advice, and your vision will resonate with your people and be more useful in driving their future actions.

Having formed a clear and compelling vision, you need to communicate it effectively to build and sustain support. A great idea communicated badly is consigned to the scrap heap of your people's minds, and communication planning is a commonly overlooked part of change planning. This is a *big* mistake, as we know that most issues in the workplace stem from communication problems. Change is no different. There are a number of issues in communication during each major step in the change process that can cost dearly.

An old adage in marketing and communications says "seven times seven different ways." This means that using multiple channels and communicating multiple times will keep the vision in the forefront of people's minds. Some people are visual while others learn via written communication. Others crave more interpersonal means. In general, you should use a mix of all so that everyone has a chance to "hear" the message in their preferred way of receiving communication.

Offer opportunities for interaction, remembering that important messages should be personally delivered and that live communication allows people to ask questions and respond. Regular opportunities for dialogue act as a release valve. They allow you to address concerns as they arise so that people can move past them and continue to remain engaged. Consider your potential communication streams: emails, intranet, social media, memorandums, group meetings, one-on-one discussions, and live audio or video calls may all be options. Remember that some are more impersonal than others and that you shouldn't use them to communicate emotional content. Be intentional about how, how often, and to whom you communicate.

You may need to adapt your vision communication based on audience. To support the vision, a group of managers may need detailed communication to satisfy their desire for review and analysis. You want your managers aligned and supportive before visions cascade down through the organization. On that basis, you also need to consider the order of communication based on your audience, particularly if the change is broad in scope. Create a communication plan and schedule that accompanies each main step in the change process.

- *Do you remember to create a clear, simple vision of the "better tomorrow" you wish to communicate during times of change?*
- *Do you create a vision communication plan and schedule so that you are intentional about how, how often, and to whom you communicate?*
- *Do you use multiple forums (one-one one conversations, group meetings, intranet, newsletters, memos, etc.) and communicate the vision multiple times on each channel?*

ADDRESS CHANGE RESISTANCE

One source of resistance is based on the organization's record of past successes and failures in implementing change, which will color your people's views regarding management's competence and the odds of success. If team members have a dim view of management's ability based on past initiatives, or the relationship isn't a good one, they're unlikely to lend their support. This is why credibility is such an important aspect of the relationship between leaders and their people. If your people don't have much belief in you, then they're not going to follow you willingly down a road they believe leads to nowhere.

Fear is the primary emotion causing change resistance. The current state has several advantages in our minds; it's known, predictable, comfortable, and we "understand the rules of the game." The status quo might not be as "good" as it could be—it may even be somewhat insane—but it's the crazy we know and that has some appeal. Change is uncertain. Our transition journey isn't a road yet built or known, and we're also unsure whether the desired destination will ever be reached.

As humans, we're inclined to "fill in the blanks" of an unknown story, often creating a worst-case scenario in our minds. Just like gossip, change narratives become more and more negative the more facts and plans are replaced by conjecture. One of the important roles change communication plays is to manage the narrative rather than let it be hijacked by the dark corners of people's minds.

Anxiety is related to fear, and the emotions we feel over uncertainty, potential loss of status and expertise, the pain that change may entail, and the requirement to learn new skills can all cause stress. The natural reaction to stress is "fight or flight," where we either withdraw from participating in change and passively resist, or we actively work against it. In either case, we do it as part of an innate response to anxiety and fear, believing that both will go away if we can avoid putting ourselves in the midst of change.

Although change might be beneficial for the group, individuals can experience real loss in the process. Jobs may be eliminated or changed in ways that reduce prestige, authority, and autonomy. A loss of control over our circumstances is a common discomfort during change. There's an emotional loss felt too when "experts" lose their sense of self-esteem by having to start again as a novice in the new reality. Staff more deeply affected by the change will have more potential resistance to it simply because there's more at stake for them.

Work overload and emotional exhaustion can be factors in resistance. Today, the expectation is that work continues as normal and there's no loss of productivity, quality, or efficiency while change is occurring. Staff members are forced not only to perform their "day job" well, but also to navigate successfully though change. It rarely happens. If it does, team members become burned out and disengaged, may feel unappreciated, and depart the company.

It's unrealistic to expect that change won't have some impact on daily operations. The question is how to minimize any negative effects. This doesn't just involve telling people to work harder or longer hours. Self-control and active focus are required to implement change because working on unfamiliar tasks requires concentration. Tasks that under the status quo became second nature and were on "autopilot" are no longer so under the new way. This can drain us.

The amount of advance notice that people receive and the degree of their influence over change are both factors affecting their resistance level. No one likes being blindsided by change, which includes changes that have already been decided upon elsewhere. The courage to talk about any change, including imposed change, is a mark of respect for your people. You signal that they're valuable enough to be kept informed, listened to, and their concerns addressed. The lack of notice sends the opposite message to them, and resistance is the price of their suffering that indignity. In addition, where individuals have a voice in shaping change, they are more likely to be supportive of the future they are helping to craft.

While there are explainable reasons why team members resist change, there are also a variety of reasons people embrace change. Change can bring opportunity—to learn new skills, take on new challenges, work with new teams or on new projects, take on a new job, and expand influence and responsibility. It can bring variety to work and energize the team. The ability to participate in a new reality is a part of renewal and innovation, which can be exciting. Where benefits are clearly apparent, change can resolve problems and help people realize actual gains. With a natural human focus on the negative, it's easy to forget the myriad of appeals that change can hold for our team members.

- ***Do you provide as much advance notice of impending change as is practical, or are your people commonly blind-sided by changes at the last minute?***
- ***Do you seek to understand the potential causes of your people's resistance and begin to address them?***
- ***Do you discuss the opportunities that change may bring for your people in both group and one-on-one settings?***

KNOW YOUR PEOPLE

If you want to work through change more effectively, then knowing your people well will help. Discovery Learning Inc. has described three primary types of participants in change. Knowing which category your people fall into during any particular change initiative may help you adapt your leadership to help change succeed. The first group are the *Conservers*. These individuals are more comfortable with gradual change and those that maintain the current structure of teams and work. Conservers respect the status quo and tradition and tend to be disciplined, organized, and detail-oriented. They may also appear as stubborn and skeptical.

The *Originators* operate on the other end of the spectrum. They continually challenge the status quo, asking, "Why do we do it this way?" They're enthusiastic change advocates who are comfortable with rapid and radical change. They may be persuasive and have good presentation skills. Originators tend to have less regard for tradition, rules, and process, and are less organized and concerned with detail. They also may have unrealistic expectations about the positive impact of change.

The middle group are the *Pragmatists*, which is where most people most of the time tend to fall regarding any given change. This group is flexible, realistic, and practical in its attitude toward change. Its members can also help bridge gaps in understanding between the Originators and Conservers. If you persuade the Pragmatists that you have a reasonable change plan and that change is beneficial for them, they're likely to be supportive.

The Conservers are commonly confused with *Resistors*, who are different. Conservers are not resisting the change for its own sake, although it may sound like it. The Conservers will ask lots of questions that may seem annoying, but they hold an important role in change. I would be concerned for any change group that does not have at least one Conserver in it. The Conservers pose questions like: "Do you have a change plan?" "What about a communication plan for the change?" "Are there goals and milestones?" "How will we know that the change has been successful?" "What about the downstream effects on our vendors, employees, and customers?" These questions don't signal resistance; they indicate a desire to see change done once and done well.

Conservers may uncover gaps in change planning, missing details, and issues we failed to consider as leaders. All of this is valuable information that slows down rushed change and helps make it more successful. As the Conservers are disciplined, organized, and detail-oriented, they also play a valuable role in the change project team—perhaps even leading the implementation.

Originators play a different, but also valuable, role. They're advocates for change that get the process started by questioning the status quo and generating awareness and enthusiasm for change. They may act as the face of change during the early stages and keep others engaged as change unfolds. Because of their lack of focus on process and detail they're unlikely to have a leadership role in the implementation phase, however, where detail becomes increasingly important.

The Pragmatists form the core change participant group, and their realistic, flexible approach can be real assets to the team. They may act as facilitators for understanding and compromise between the Conservers and Originators. When you know the part all your people may play in change—as well as potential gaps in their approaches to change—you can more effectively position them to play to their strengths and maximize their talents.

Some "key players" also play important roles in the field. These people are often de facto leaders or mentors on teams—those who may not have a formal leadership title but are experienced "go-to" people who their coworkers respect. Other key players may be those with specialist skills (i.e., technical specialists, or those with financial/accounting, HR, quality/risk, or other specific expertise). People with access to important resources needed for the change (for example, IT, accounting/finance, project office, etc.) also play important roles. Anyone may fit into the role of a key player depending upon the nature of the change initiative.

Use the key players you've identified. People are social creatures. This is why the concept of role modeling is so prevalent in human psychology. People replicate behavior they observe and are particularly sensitive to the actions of those they respect and admire. When in doubt, people look for environmental cues about what steps to take, and role models provide direction. When leaders know their team well, including who the "go-to" respected members of the team are, it allows them to focus energy on building advocacy among the key players.

With the Originators and Key Players (some of whom might fall into the Pragmatist or Conserver categories) supporting the cause, others may be won over by the power of numbers. If there's a respected Conserver in the group, addressing their concerns and issues early may help too. If you can convince one of the influential skeptics in the group then winning over the rest becomes less difficult. You need the key players on board. Without their expertise, resources, and credibility, influencing hearts and minds and making change a reality become much more difficult.

Many leaders mistakenly think that the sheer power of their own personality and their authority will win the day without additional help. Even the most respected change leaders don't have great relationships with literally everyone. Advocates may use a different approach to get the message across more effectively in the minds of certain team members, and they may have credibility already built up in areas where you might be lacking.

By understanding each team member's motivators, this can be factored into the conversation about the gains and losses of change in a way that will better resonate with them. This will drive them to see that the transition process is less painful—or has greater benefit—than remaining the same. Avoiding pain is often a more powerful drive than seeking pleasure, so when change is not a matter of crisis but opportunity, the benefits need to be clear and significant to motivate people. Remember that people have strong internal drivers for autonomy, inclusion, significance, and empowerment. You will be wise to try to fulfill them by also considering the roles your team members will play in the upcoming change process.

Another factor unique to times of change is also important to consider. Tension exists between the stress of learning new skills and procedures and that involved with survival. You can use this tension to drive change forward:

> Change will require unlearning old ways and learning new ones, and the result of learning anxiety is to inhibit change to a greater or lesser degree … To motivate people to make a desired change, it is necessary to create sufficient survival anxiety to destabilize the current situation and drive them forward. At the same time it is necessary to support people in such a way that they feel safe enough to learn effectively— that their learning anxiety (which would hold them back) is kept as

low as possible, and certainly lower than the survival anxiety. (King, Sidhu, Skelsey, and Smith, *The Effective Change Manager's Handbook*, p. 22)

Where survival anxiety outweighs that associated with learning "the new way," drive for change occurs as long as you can demonstrate change as a credible solution. Stoking that anxiety during the course of creating and communicating vision will help garner support and attention among your people. Whatever your approach, consider individual internal motivators when crafting and communicating your change vision. You'll gather more momentum for the initiative in doing so.

- *Of those people on your team, do you know who the Originators, Pragmatists, and Conservers are likely to be during the upcoming change?*
- *Do you consider the parts each team member will play during change initiatives based upon this information?*
- *Do you use individual motivators to drive change amongst your team members?*

CREATE AND COMMUNICATE A CHANGE PLAN

Change requires leadership *and* management, so we must also attend to the details. This means planning, scheduling, allocating resources, managing workflow, and considering the order of activities. If change is to be successful then there's no avoiding this stage of the process, as Heath and Heath also contend in *Switch*: "Many leaders pride themselves on setting high level direction: *I'll set the vision and stay out of the details*. It's true that a compelling vision is critical. But it's not enough. Big-picture, hands-off leadership isn't likely to work in a change situation, because the hardest part of change—the paralyzing part—is precisely in the details ... Ambiguity is the enemy. Any successful change requires a translation of ambiguous goals into concrete behaviors" (pp. 53-54).

Staff discussions may have generated ideas. Now is the time to consider them, speaking with your people to better understand the advantages and drawbacks of each before a change solution is chosen. Even when change comes from above, the freedom—and the obligation—to ensure that the change is implemented successfully allows you to create the change plan within your team. The message is simple though: "Prior planning prevents poor performance." You need to have a plan, and that means you have to now choose a solution option that is going to guide successful change.

When considering your solution options, you'll have to weigh up impacts upon the various stakeholders. The first is the effect on the customer. They are the reason the business exists, and the change's effect on them must be given priority consideration. Are you going to maintain those customers who are already happy? Will indifferent or unhappy customers be more content and attracted to the organization? Will the change help win and maintain more business? Will the change make it easier or harder for customers to do business with the company? How is cost, quality, or service delivery impacted?

You also need to carefully weigh the potential impacts on employees. Often, leaders assume that staff will just magically adapt somehow and work through the change without much consideration to how change will impact their feelings about the organization and their work experience. Overall, will the change make the work experience easier or more difficult for your people? Will happy and productive employees continue to be content? Will unhappy employees be more, or less, content after the change? What effect, overall, will the change have on the engagement, productivity, and retention or your people? How will they maintain their productivity and carry out their change roles successfully at the same time? Will they need to learn different skills and adapt to new workflows?

A commonly overlooked area is the impact on vendors/business partners. As you engage with them to help make your business successful, changes you make may fundamentally affect your relationships with them. Will the vendors need to change their systems or processes in response to the changes you're implementing in your own organization? Will the change affect whether the vendor will still be suitable to use in future? Will it require a substantially different way of working together to deliver products and services? Will the vendor's people need to take on new skills or knowledge to adapt to the change?

It's very important to consider the downstream effects on these crucial stakeholder groups, and the business in general, to plan and execute change well. Like ripples in the water, one change will cause others to become necessary, so you need a thorough and structured approach to change planning.

Build milestones into your change plan, particularly if the change initiative is lengthier, complex, or requires a number of relatively distinct stages. Milestones play a number of important functions that help you move change forward. First, they provide evidence of progress. There's a reason mile markers are sprayed on roads during long running races; they tell participants, "You're making progress; here's how far you've come!" When we have visible signs of progress, we take heart from it; it strengthens our resolve to complete the rest of the journey.

Second, the visible signs of progress provide evidence to senior stakeholders that they should continue to support the initiative. They also prove to skeptics that the plan is working and they need to jump on board and support the change or risk getting left behind. Third, the celebrating of milestone accomplishments helps maintain morale and motivation. It's an opportunity to recognize progress and appreciate your team's work.

There's basic psychology around motivation that asserts we weigh cost, benefit, and chances of attainment—a risk/reward analysis—in our heads. That helps us weigh the appeal of the reward (internal or external), the pain of achieving it, and our chances of reaching the goal. Ask someone who has never run a triathlon to participate in an Ironman-distance race within a month, and you are likely to get a refusal. Ask the same person to try a sprint-distance triathlon with three months, and you may persuade them.

Milestones help us break down a seemingly insurmountable achievement into bite-size chunks ("eating the elephant one bite at a time") that we can conquer. Taking a long-term goal and increasing immediacy through milestones helps us pressure the team to achieve near-term objectives. Creating some reasonable level of tension can be useful for success.

Setting out goals and measurables is an equally important part of change planning. How will you know whether the change initiative has been successful? The answer comes from achieving the measurables. Change performance is just another aspect of performance management, after all. In this case, the KPIs you set should not only push forward the change process itself but also measure the effects resulting from the implemented change. You can then assess the ROI of change using metrics related to productivity, efficiency, timeliness, customer service, and financial performance.

Measurables related to process are useful milestone markers; those related to change effects are used post-implementation. Research shows that the documentation of goals has a positive effect on their achievement. Cameron and Green, in *Making Sense of Change Management*, also assert this, referencing a study of Yale University graduates over a period of twenty years.

The study found that the primary variable between the top 3 percent (who were wealthier than the other 97 percent combined) was that they had clearly articulated and written goals (p. 27).

Training is a commonly overlooked aspect of change planning. For the most part, it is at best affiliated with the plan but separate from it. Good change plans integrate learning and development initiatives, ensuring that learning needs are assessed and clearly articulated. Design, development and delivery considerations are specifically outlined, including defining the audience, order of training (typically managers first to address supervisor questions and build coaching capacity for the field), schedule, and deadlines.

Training KPIs are set and integrated into the overall measurables for the change initiative, but also using learning-specific metrics to assess training impact. If your initiative is small scale and within your team, don't overcomplicate it, however. Instead, have a plan that you can actually implement rather than one that looks perfect on paper but will never come to fruition. This includes using KPIs, but not more than are needed.

Training is an investment in people, and it will require their time and attention. They need to be allowed sufficient time and resources to properly train to help make the change successful. You must ensure you commit to training, remembering that staff can't be asked to train on top of their regular duties without the expectation that accommodations will need to be made for them.

While we all seek to minimize the negative impact on productivity while staff are away from their regular duties, just assuming that they'll willingly and enthusiastically put in the extra hours and effort to learn is naïve. In addition, short-changing training by abbreviating or rushing it is a common mistake. You may woefully underestimate the time and effort it takes to change habits built up over months and years of daily work, believing that a day or week's training (often with little follow-up instruction) will unwind old habits and quickly build and sustain new ones.

Change, by definition, implies the end of one thing and the beginning of something new. Commonly, we overlook the fact that, in addition to reasons of comfort with the status quo and fear of the unknown, there are other strands of emotional connection to the way things are today. Just like people will help make today's change initiative a reality, they were likely also players in the last change initiative that became the status quo. There is pride associated with that, and the implication that the house we built is no longer adequate may be met with some resentment and defensiveness.

Be aware that it's going to take time for people to move emotionally past the loss of the current state. People have a stake, for various reasons, in the way things currently are. Don't just expect them to abandon it without having feelings about the transition, and don't badmouth the status quo that others helped build. It, too, was new and untried at one point and also considered an improvement over what came before it.

> Many managers, in their enthusiasm for a future that is going to be better than the past, ridicule or demean the old way of doing things. In doing so they consolidate resistance against the transition because people identify with the way things used to be and thus feel that their self-worth is at stake whenever the past is attacked ... Endings occur more easily if people can take a bit of the past with them. You are trying to disengage people from it, not stamp it out like an infection. And in particular, you don't want to make people feel blamed for having been part of it. (Bridges and Bridges, *Managing Transitions*, pp. 39-40)

Addressing risk must also be built into your change plan. This is particularly true with wide-ranging changes and those where the cost of failure is high. Using pilot groups and user acceptance testing helps. Pilot groups can help identify implementation issues and provide valuable feedback to fine-tune the change initiative. When mistakes are made, you'd rather have them be on a small scale and in a controlled environment than laid bare across the entire organization. The damage incurred to your reputation and credibility when the company has to unwind a poorly executed change can be significant.

Pilot groups can become advocates for the change if the exercise is successful, and that can be a valuable tool to maintain change momentum. Start with a pilot group located where the change is most likely to be successful, given other factors within and outside the business. Use risk management methodologies and the tools at your disposal to assess where risk lies and how to address it as part of change planning.

In the change plan, address four fundamental areas: 1) what has been done before and will continue to be done, 2) what was done before that is now changing, 3) what is new; something never done before that will be done in the future, and 4) what was done before that is to be stopped. It's important to address these areas because it puts the change in perspective. When people are unclear about what direction to go in, they freeze or go back to the way things used to be done—which is comfortable and familiar. Minimize the chances of anything but forward progress by making these four areas clear. This also helps you avoid confusion, frustration, and wasted effort.

People regularly lose perspective during a change initiative, thinking that most everything is changing and adding unnecessarily to their emotional baggage and stress. We've all thought our world was turned upside down at some point until some sage individual helped us understand that the earth was still round and the sun would still rise and set each day. Let people ground themselves in what remains the same before you explain the other three areas of change.

So you've addressed the *what* of change in the plan; now you need to explain *how* changes are occurring. This means explaining the main steps to change in detail, supported by workflow diagrams, process maps, and procedures to aid your people and provide them a reference guide. Think again of the *what* as the destination and the *how* as the roadmap to guide the journey to it. You can tell someone who has never travelled that Paris, Tokyo, or New York is the destination, but if they don't have a guiding force, you just have dream. Give them a GPS, a map, or a tour guide.

People also need to know their *role* in the journey. Even if they have a destination and a map, if they don't see their name on the list to get on the bus, outlining which seat they occupy, they won't step on board. Are they the driver? Navigator? Tour guide? Mechanic? You have to explain what role each person plays so that they understand what activities they, specifically, need to undertake and what procedures and workflows apply to them.

The larger, riskier, and more complex the change initiative is, the more critical detailed change planning becomes. This also means that changes not fitting into these categories shouldn't be overengineered. Having a plan is always better than having none, but make sure the plan fits the change and acknowledge that not every single move in change can, or should, be scripted. People know how to run between the mile markers and signs posting a change of direction, so allow them freedom to do so. Don't overcomplicate matters and make change more stressful for your team than it already is. Make the plan only as detailed as it needs to be in order to successfully execute it—but no more than that.

Change is primarily an individual and emotional—not procedural—transition for your people. Just showing you have the "right" solution and a plan to implement it successfully isn't enough. Be prepared to deal with the emotional journeys of each team member along the way, which your plan can't account for. Planning is a *management* skill, whereas emotional intelligence and counseling are facets of *leadership* expertise and can't be scripted.

When you consider where to start a change implementation, if it concerns a wide-ranging change across the organization, start with the areas that have the fewest environmental and other challenges. Nothing breeds success like success, and seeing the plan come to fruition will help you build change momentum.

The natural tendency of leaders to take charge can lead to self-isolating behaviors. Remember that people want to be the primary author of their lives, and if you try to carry the weight of the world on your shoulders, like the story of Atlas, you risk not only change failure but also damaging the relationships with your people along the way. As Heifetz and Linsky stated, "it's tempting to go it alone when leading a change initiative. There's no one to dilute your ideas or share the glory, and it's often just plain exciting. It's also foolish. You need to recruit partners, people who can help protect you from attacks and who can point out potentially fatal flaws in your strategy or initiative. Moreover, you are far less vulnerable when you are out on the point with a bunch of folks rather than alone" (from the article "A Survival Guide for Leaders" by Heifetz and Linsky in Harvard Business Review Press, *On Change Management*, p. 104). You have to take people with you because a main aim of change is to aid others in managing their own individual transitions.

- *Do you consider the effect upon customers, employees, and vendors/partners when creating and implementing change plans?*
- *Do you integrate milestones and training plans into your overall change plan?*
- *Do you consider how you will manage risk during the change, including where you will implement the plan first and the use of pilot groups and user acceptance testing?*

IMPLEMENT THE CHANGE PLAN

Business project graveyards are littered with plans that failed to be utilized. Sometimes, valid reasons revolving around changes in circumstance led to abandoning projects. In other cases, leaders who spent time agonizing over the construction of a plan failed to follow the script, letting the tide of activities overtake them. Plans have to be adaptable, but you can't adapt them if you don't use them in the first place. Ensure they're implemented as you had intended.

Remember the issues with what has been termed "the neutral zone." You need to monitor the transitions of each team member through it in order to make change progress. The neutral zone is a stage of transition where individuals have let go of the status quo—which was known, comfortable, and something they were competent at—and are now in a state where they aren't yet comfortable or proficient at the new way of doing things. It can be both stressful and exhilarating, and it's the point at which our emotions run highest once we've taken the leap of faith toward change.

The neutral zone has perils, and it isn't someplace for your people to dwell in for long. These dangers are something that Bridges and Bridges also explain in *Managing Transitions* (pp. 46-47). They include the feeling of vulnerability where we aren't yet grounded in the new way, which leads to rising anxiety and a potential drop in motivation to help achieve the change goal. Attention turns instead to coping and self-preservation, drawing emotional resources and focus inward and away from change activity. Productivity can drop and absenteeism rises. When people lose their bearings, they also try anything to ground themselves once more. This includes attempting to do work in both the new and old ways or regressing back to doing only the familiar because it's comfortable.

Help your people by ensuring your change plan minimizes time in the neutral zone via the implementation of training, procedures, workflows, and other resources. Monitor their usage during implementation to quickly identify those who are struggling. The resistance you encounter may be a lack of clarity people are experiencing over what to do next during the change, and an indication that their time in the neutral zone is becoming perilous for them.

The plan never goes perfectly, because circumstances have likely already changed between the time you created the change plan and the time you implemented it. Different players, changed business priorities, and internal and external influences have moved on. In response, be prepared to adapt the change plan as you go. To overcome new and unforeseen obstacles, you may have to add/change the action steps, order of actions, schedules, deadlines, roles, and other aspects.

A stubborn insistence on sticking to the original plan when the need for adaptation was clear has doomed countless initiatives in business.

Help to carve a new path for your people when it's clear the one you initially intended won't lead to success. As Heath and Heath stated about molding the environment in *Switch*, "if you want people to change, you can provide clear direction (Rider) or boost their motivation and determination (Elephant). Alternatively, you can simply make the journey easier. Create a steep downhill slope and give them a push. Remove some friction from the trail. Scatter around lots of signs to tell them they're getting close" (p. 181).

Use those milestones. They'll allow you to assess performance and celebrate interim achievements that keep your team energized. Get your people feeling an early sense of accomplishment and you'll build the courage to continue along the path and resilience to overcome setbacks and obstacles. Success breeds self-esteem and fuels the journey you're asking your people to make. Be regular with your interactions so you can observe and address issues as they occur. Encourage your people to also reach out for help when they encounter issues and are unsure of how to deal with them.

A critical and unforgiving attitude is soul-crushing for your people—who will hasten their way toward the door—and inhibits innovation, accountability, and risk-taking. When people fear being crucified for any mistake, their energy focuses on self-preservation and risk-avoidance. This does not help the organization and team improve, innovate, and change. "An organizational culture dominated by fear is incapable of serious change. Fear encourages everyone to avoid risks, hunker down, and keep their mouths shut—even to conceal disappointing results ... Employees at all levels must feel free to challenge the status quo, identify problems, and suggest solutions—even when their views conflict with those of the leadership. They must also feel free to try new things without fear of retribution if they fail" (Harvard Business Press, *Managing Change and Transition*, pp. 28-29).

- *Do you follow the plan you've created to use for change implementation, or allow circumstances to overwhelm you and cause it to be easily discarded?*
- *Do you use policies, procedures, process maps, workflows, and training to shorten the time your people spend in "the neutral zone"?*
- *Are you flexible, and review and adapt your plan to circumstances that arise during implementation itself?*

INSTITUTIONALIZE CHANGE; "MAKE IT STICK"

Change initiatives are sometimes prematurely declared "complete." In the rush for progress, leaders are tempted to declare victory when the procedural steps of change have been completed. Often, this happens without an honest assessment of how the initiative went against the ultimate purposes for which it was implemented. This can only be done over time, through a process of monitoring and measurement. Resist the temptation to become complacent in sight of the finish line by not following through to make sure change truly 'sticks' within the organization.

One element you can control to maintain change is the physical environment. Rearranging workspaces to support the new way of doing things and removing the tools that were used by 'the old way' guides changed behavior. Process and procedures are also important levers to maintain change. Replace old policies and procedures with new ones that act as reference guides for consistently doing things "the new way." Process maps, workflow diagrams, and checklists are resources to aid the change.

As Heath and Heath explained in *Switch*, checklists are not something to fear but instead to be embraced as a change aid, stating that "people fear checklists because they see them as dehumanizing—maybe because they associate them with the exhaustive checklists that allow inexperienced teenagers to operate fast-food chains successfully. If they think something is simple enough to be put in a checklist, a monkey can do it. Well, if that's true, grab a pilot checklist and try your luck with a 747" (p. 222).

The aim of these resources is to help build behavioral triggers. This is how habits are created, and when we have habits we have "unconscious competence" where people execute without having to think much and call on their emotional control and discipline. This is the muscle memory that elite athletes call upon unconsciously to achieve. It's the replacement of thought with "instinct" that football (soccer) stars Lionel Messi, Cristiano Ronaldo, and Mia Hamm have used to put the ball in the back of the net. It's how LeBron James, Michael Jordan, Kobe Bryant, and Maya Moore poured in shot after shot to win basketball championships. It's how Michael Schumacher and Lewis Hamilton steered their cars to repeated victory on the F1 circuit.

When people are asked to acknowledge their understanding and commitment to the new policies and procedures, additional accountability to support change is built. Archive old policies and procedures so they're no longer readily available to your people and replace them with the new, easily accessible documents. In addition, review and discuss the new policies and procedures so that team members are clear on actions to be taken and their part in them. The timing and manner of communicating and reviewing new policies and procedures should be part of communication planning.

Auditing is another resource commonly used to help institutionalize change. As we've already discussed, follow-up performs useful functions, including building accountability for adapting to change and using the new processes, systems, and structures as intended. It also helps uncover training and support needs, which should improve results further once addressed. Lastly, inspection helps you analyze how performance is faring versus the KPIs set for the change initiative. Measurables can help ensure the change endures, as what gets measured gets done.

Training is another means of institutionalizing change. Training can shorten the time your people spend in the neutral zone, speed up adaptation, and support improved productivity and results. Training is commonly minimized, as it's mistakenly assumed that creating and distributing new policies, procedures, and process maps is enough and that staff will self-teach around these reference resources. This only adds to their stress load, and ten people self-teaching is going to produce less consistent results than learning delivered by one trainer whose understanding of the material and objectives is more thorough. Build training in, and make sure it's organized and professional rather than a trial-and-error learning approach that regularly plagues change initiatives.

The emotional drivers that you leveraged to support the move toward change also help sustain it. Acknowledging behavior that complements and supports change, celebrating change success, allowing people input and responsibility in supporting the new way, and providing people greater autonomy under the new state all can help your cause. Emotional levers have the greatest raw power to start change, help people move through transition, and sustain the new way.

You must apply all of these resources over a period of time post-implementation. It could be months or even longer before change can truly be said to have "stuck" and become part of the organization's fabric. Don't become complacent as the weeks wear on and continue to observe, inspect, and assess to see if what actually resulted from your change initiative was what you intended.

- *What resources or "levers" do you use today to institutionalize change on your team?*
- *Do you declare victory too early during times of change or take time to follow up, audit, and measure change effects to ensure change had the successful impact you intended?*
- *Do you use the power of your people's internal motivators to ensure that they help sustain the implemented change?*

A WORD ON CHANGE COMMUNICATION

We've spoken about how important communication is to leadership success. The communication plan, whether integrated into the change plan for larger, more complex change initiatives or outlined more simply for small-scope changes, is a very important factor in change success.

Set communications objectives, and bear in mind some basic tenets of change communication. The first is that the process should be two-way. You should want team members' information, feedback, and ideas. They can be invaluable in helping regulate and use emotion to support change, plan more effectively, and obtain better results. Build opportunities for give-and-take throughout the steps in the change process, and allocate time and attention to listen to your people. You might also need to tailor your messages depending on the audience. While the core of the messages remains the same, different groups may have unique priorities, concerns, and communication norms to address in order to obtain support.

People appreciate transparency, so be as open as you can. Where information gaps exist, people will fill them in with rumor and innuendo, which typically are negative or worst-case scenario stories that then spread. If you don't control the narrative, the grapevine will instead.

When you communicate, use multiple forums and instances to relay important messages. Your people will have varied communication preferences, and they'll begin to assimilate the message after receiving it several times. Some people will read communications such as memos and emails carefully, while others will bin them, preferring some form of interactive communication instead.

Messages must be straightforward and simple. Don't overload people with information in long emails, memos, or town hall meetings packed with unnecessary detail. You're only going to create stress and lose the interest of your audience. Use visuals to aid your communication, as they're often simple, yet impactful ways to get your points across.

Section 7

DEVELOPING OTHERS

P eople are motivated to come to work and stay with their employers for a variety of reasons. Desire for personal growth, learning, challenge, and achievement can be very strong internal motivators—and all of those are related to learning and development. If you're a leader you're also a developer. This means that you must invest time, effort, and resources into molding others to contribute to collective goals and enabling them to grow their skills and careers as your team's achievements grow.

Learning opportunities are not a value-add for your people; they're a prerequisite to attract and retain talent in today's job market, particularly based on current generational work preferences. If you don't develop your people, they will find another leader who will. The collective energy and intelligence of your team are precious resources. The competitor down the road doesn't have them, and they can't be easily duplicated. Your role is to find a way to uncover both and nurture them so your team members experience growth and success.

A key to great leadership lies in the ability to identify and develop talent. It's a crucial factor in your own leadership success. If you lead others and don't have an interest in coaching and developing, then you must rethink whether you're in the right role for the sake of your own happiness and success and that of your team. They'll underachieve versus their potential and likely find the experience of your leadership unenjoyable – while they remain in the job. You're also likely to find your own leadership experience less than fulfilling.

Investment in people is important to their engagement, productivity, and retention. The Gallup organization, which has been surveying the workforce for many years, has found that having someone who encourages employee growth and development is vitally important to workforce engagement. Without it, only 1 percent of employees achieve real engagement, while two-thirds of employees who have someone encouraging their development are classified as "engaged" (Harter and Wagner, *12: The Elements of Great*

Managing, p. 81). This is a massive difference-maker that means leaders, in only the rarest cases, engage their staff without them having a supporter for their growth and development. The message is clear: If you want to capture your people's hearts and minds, you must provide them growth and development opportunities.

Time and attention are some of the few things that we cannot produce more of. No matter what experience or expertise individuals have, time is the great equalizer. All of us have the same amount of it to spend each day, so we choose carefully how to allocate this most precious resource. As John Maxwell stated, "we live in a fast-paced, demanding world, and time is a difficult thing to give. It is a leader's most valuable commodity ... When you give of yourself, it benefits you, the organization, and the receiver. Nurturing leaders must maintain a giving attitude. Norman Vincent Peale expressed it well when he said that the man who lives for himself is a failure; the man who lives for others has achieved true success" (Maxwell, *Developing the Leaders around You*, pp. 68-69).

Nothing signals investment in our people like spending time with them, particularly one-on-one. When that time includes a focus on coaching and professional growth, it can be particularly rewarding for both you and your people. The counsel, knowledge, and experience that you impart to others directly are an invaluable part of their learning and development. Allocated time demonstrates your commitment to your people and interest in seeing them progress and succeed in their careers.

Your time and attention is important, but because it's limited you have to choose how and when to provide it to best effect. There's typically an array of other learning and development resources, both within and outside your organization, that you can use to help your team members develop. These resources, together with your personal coaching, can be part of an effective portfolio of development resources for them.

From mentoring and 360-degree feedback processes to job shadowing, interim and project assignments, experiential learning, classroom training and webinars, and self-study, many ways of helping your people learn and grow exist. With a little forethought and creativity, you can produce an effective training plan for your team members that also engages and develops others along the way. There are also excellent resources outside your organization to help develop your people, and they may even bring back some innovative ideas along the way that have worked for other companies.

In the long term, a development mindset is the only sustainable choice for your leadership foundation. As you develop others you'll find they are willing to repay you by sharing the burden of your position, taking on additional duties and responsibilities that in turn grow their expertise and prepare them for the next step in their own careers.

ONBOARDING

Onboarding is a crucial activity that learning and development plays a substantial role in. The manner in which new people are integrated into the team and organization plays a crucial role in their future productivity, engagement, and retention. There's substantial evidence to support the importance of onboarding to employee experience. Harpelund, Hojberg, and Nielsen, in *Onboarding* (pp. 1-2) reference research that shows how proper onboarding can increase employee commitment, reduce time to productivity and stress, and increase retention and job satisfaction. They state that 25 percent of new hires typically leave within twelve months of hire, and 46 percent leave within eighteen months.

When you consider the significant amount of time, effort, and money taken to recruit and hire new team members, the potential for half or more of them to leave within eighteen months is a massive drain on productivity and resources. Some studies indicate that "full" productivity isn't reached until six or more months of service, as is the break-even point where staff are effectively paying for themselves via their productivity levels. The stakes are high for organizational expenses and efficiency via onboarding. In addition to the cost of lost productivity (perhaps the largest onboarding expense), ineffective onboarding can negatively affect employee engagement and retention and the company's employer reputation in the marketplace—which only makes it harder and more costly to recruit in the future.

As an immediate supervisor, you own the onboarding experience of your new staff. Onboarding is neither a training activity nor an HR function. Staff in these functions have only a supporting role to play. Onboarding is an organizational function, and you must take primary responsibility for the onboarding of your new staff. After all, they'll become members of your team and will affect its productivity, dynamics, and results.

Structured onboarding programs benefit you and your organization. Whether or not they exist in your business today, you have an obligation as leader to plan, implement, and follow through with onboarding effectively. Whether onboarding is a memorable or infamous experience in the mind of your new team member starts and ends with the person in the mirror. You own it, so own it.

Onboarding is one of those seminal activities that separates true leaders from supervisors merely warming the chairs with their backsides. The former engage heavily in the process to make sure their new people are set up for success on the job. The latter are happy to abdicate their responsibility and attempt to be passengers in the process, hoping others will take on the hard work of integrating new people and working them toward "full" productivity.

From the moment a candidate says "yes" to the job offer and begins to excitedly envision a future career in your organization, as a leader you should turn your attention to their proper onboarding. Your new hire is coming in with stress, fear, and uncertainty—but also a great deal of drive, enthusiasm, and potential. The quality of onboarding will determine whether the latter is captured or lost. New hires are hypersensitive to the things they see, hear, and experience. It's likely that within the first four to six weeks they've already determined whether they can build a career with you or if the job will just be a holdover until they find something more attractive. It's been said that "you never get a second chance to make a good first impression." You don't have much time to make that good impression on the people you've worked so hard in prior weeks and months to hire.

> … readiness is an element of good onboarding. It means a lot that things seem to be ready and someone is looking after your back. It can be very simple things like the physical workspace being ready. And that the tools which the new hire needs are ready, whether it's a hammer or an iPad. The same applies to the business card, the phone number and the passwords and codes that the new hire is dependent upon. This is important because it plays into the employee's experience of feeling welcome. The fact that the practical conditions are in place, of course, also affects the actual efficiency of the new hire, but from an emotional perspective, it plays a special role by showing the company to be a good host. (Harpelund, Hojberg, and Nielsen, *Onboarding*, p. 68)

Often, managers succumb to the temptation to rush a new hire in for their first day of work. Why? Because for some reason they believe that taking a few more days to properly organize and plan for a new hire's arrival is too inconvenient. The result is often a negative onboarding experience for the new employee, or at very best one that's mediocre. Don't give in to this temptation. If your organization has a preparation checklist for onboarding, use it. If not, create one. Creating a simple guide for the most important preparation activities allows you to significantly impact the quality of onboarding. It doesn't take much time to create, and once you have a checklist you can use this repeatable process with future new hires.

Obvious areas to concentrate on include the ordering of equipment, supplies, business cards, uniforms, and systems/building access. Give your IT department the proper amount of lead time to do so, and they'll try their best to ensure that you have the hardware and access you need for the new hire's first day of employment. Remember that they have projects and workloads too. Last-minute requests where they in turn must rely on the speed of outside suppliers and other external circumstances put the onboarding experience at risk from the very beginning. Ensuring that the physical workspace is set up (desk, chair, phone, monitor, supplies, etc.) is also important.

Ensure that you build in touchpoints such as a welcome email or check-in call with your new hire the week before their first day, and even a welcome card on the workstation. These things go a long way toward making them feel welcome. Announcing the future arrival of the new hire to the team and other stakeholders in the organization (including HR and training) is also important so they can also prepare themselves for the new hire's arrival.

Creating an hour-by-hour, day-by-day schedule for your new hire for the first few weeks of employment is another crucial aspect of successful onboarding. Leaders commonly fall down here, failing to plan the new hire's early days on the job. As a result, onboarding appears disorganized, disjointed, and a less-than-efficient use of everyone's time. This exercise might take you a little longer as a leader, but the return on this investment of time is significant.

Items to schedule during the first several weeks may include: 1) the induction/orientation session, often coordinated by HR or training, 2) introductory meetings with stakeholders, including internal customers, mentors, and those the new hire should build ties with to perform their role successfully, 3) classroom training sessions on systems/procedures,

4) regular one-on-one check-in sessions with you to discuss progress and issues (should be twice weekly at a minimum in the first month, then at least weekly thereafter during onboarding), 5) open time for self-study and review of material, 6) assigned eLearning, 7) job shadowing or other side-by-side time spent with experienced staff, 8) participation in group meetings, and 9) sessions spent with you as leader personally training and coaching them.

Using a schedule allows you to organize and pace training so that it's more effective and digestible for new hires. This is a significant concern, as overwhelming people with information not only increases their stress and confusion but also minimizes their knowledge retention. Having a list of the stakeholders the new hire will meet with, including an explanation of their relationship to the new hire's role, is also helpful. If you can take only two actions regarding orientation, make them building a checklist to prepare for a new hire's first day on the job and using a schedule template for the first several weeks. You'll improve the effectiveness of onboarding significantly via this preparation work.

When staff members are provided the schedule for several weeks of work, their stress and fear associated with uncertainty diminishes. A schedule also evidences your leadership's professionalism to the new hire right from the first day of work, which is important to their engagement in onboarding and future retention. It also helps the new hire understand where onboarding begins and "finishes," even if there are some follow-up activities in future months. A beginning and end signals when new staff are expected to be fully performing their daily duties and is important to building accountability within new team members.

People are driven by feeling. Their experience at work creates the thoughts that drive emotion, and that emotion fuels behavior. Work, as a major part of our waking lives, can't help but have emotion attached to it. So before we start checking off items on our list or fill in the daily schedules of our new hires, consider how you want them to feel as a part of these early work experiences.

As a leader, you are the shaper of reality for your people. Create one of excitement, growth, challenge, empowerment, and support, and do so as quickly as you can. New team members crave those feelings as much as you do, and as the weeks go on, excitement and anticipation for the new job wanes with onboarding mediocrity. "New hires can watch hours of video films, read the staff manual from cover to cover, have meetings with all the line managers and have ambitious career plans, all without necessarily having the slightest feeling of belonging to the organization or that they have a meaningful role in it. No matter what activities we build into our programs, onboarding is all about creating emotions" (Harpelund, Hojberg, and Nielsen, *Onboarding*, p. 9).

- *Do you properly prepare for your new hire's first day of work, using a checklist or other guide to make sure you are thorough and well-organized?*
- *Do you plan the hour-by-hour, day-by-day schedule for your new hire for the first few weeks, presenting them with a copy of the schedule on their first day and explaining it?*
- *Do you explain to the new hire who they will be meeting with as part of their onboarding and their relationship to the new hire's position?*

CONNECTING DURING ONBOARDING

Precisely because work is part of the human experience and new employment is filled with emotion, it's important that new team members build connections with those that can support them in their role. This helps them understand the expectations associated with their work and enculturates them into the organization. In addition, building friendships is part of what makes work enjoyable. It's hard to leave a workplace where our friends are—and easy to walk away from an environment in which we feel lonely and isolated. We're social beings and need connection with others. Some interesting research on this exists as it relates to employee engagement:

> According to research performed by the Gallup organization, 30% of workers polled strongly agreed that they had a best friend in the workplace. Among this group, 56% reported being engaged workers, 33% reported being unengaged, and 11% reported being actively unengaged. Compare this with the 70% of workers who didn't strongly agree that they had a best friend at work: Only 8% of this group reported being engaged employees, 63% reported being not engaged, and 29% reported being actively disengaged. (Christiansen and Stein, *Successful Onboarding*, p. 123)

Building strong social connections during onboarding can result in higher commitment, better retention, and decreased time to productivity. The relationship between effective socialization of new hires and their work engagement is very strong, and it's vital for leaders to be mindful of this when planning and carrying out onboarding. As very few jobs today are free from interaction and the requirement to build and maintain effective relationships, this aspect of onboarding must be a deliberate part of the process.

Plan for new team members to make connections with those who are important to their job performance—the coworkers on their team, others who have access to resources or specialist expertise they will need, and internal customers who will assess the effectiveness of their work. Your new team member must build ties and credibility, and experience early success that is so vital to their morale. The clock is also ticking for new hires to make an initial impression on stakeholders that proves they can positively contribute to the team.

The use of mentors, either via a formal program or informal pairing, can be a valuable part of the connection process. Mentors provide a model for behavior and answer the more routine questions that arise. Mentors can help explain issues in a different way to aid in understanding, and they offer a valuable ear to help make the transition into the new role more comfortable. Sometimes new staff are reluctant to tell you they still aren't understanding an issue or process, which may be because of how you've communicated it. Mentoring is also a valuable opportunity for more experienced staff to build their coaching skills, which is a natural prerequisite for a future leadership role.

New hires need to connect with others who may help them indirectly in their work or may share common interests and experiences. Internal interest-based committees can be one place to start, but often this is done through informal introductions and the opportunity for people to engage in casual conversations. Get to know some basics about your new team members and be perceptive enough to gauge who they may find social conversations enjoyable with. No one wants to talk work all day every day. Having those with whom we share interests and socialize makes good days even better and tough days more tolerable.

Don't just assume that connections will organically grow—germinate them through planned interactions for your new hire. You'll reap the benefits of an engaged and productive new team member. Onboarding is a very interactive process. People can't be onboarded sitting in front of a computer screen taking eLearning courses. New hires need real living, breathing guides who can empathize with, and respond to, their emotions during the crucial first few weeks of the process. They also need someone who will monitor their progress beyond that to make sure their first year experience is positive and productive.

- *Do you make connecting with others a conscious part of the onboarding process for your people?*
- *Do you connect people with others who can support them in their roles at work, or that they may find it enjoyable to socialize with?*
- *Do you make use of mentoring as a tool during the onboarding process?*

ENCULTURATION OF NEW STAFF

How do you describe the company culture to new hires and applicants? What about the culture within your business unit and team? Culture isn't an easy thing to capture and describe, but the clearer it's defined for the people who operate within it the better they can regulate their own, and others', behavior to meet its expectations. Companies that have a sharply defined and communicated culture, one that's actively maintained through daily activity and not just dusted off at annual review time for discussion, focus their resources and effort more effectively to thrive in their markets. They know who they are, what they stand for, what they are good at, and what priorities exist. Because they have clear identity and purpose, they can also better match culture to applicant preferences to ensure there's fundamental alignment between them.

Onboarding is a crucial time to delve deeper into culture to help new staff better understand and align with its expectations. This part of onboarding is often overlooked or delegated to HR, where an idealized cultural overview is sometimes communicated rather than today's reality. Don't just assume that new hires will magically "get it" with culture, picking up on the nuances of values and norms themselves without guidance.

> ... most companies do not equip managers with the tools they need to capture, distill, and ultimately help acculturate the new hire. Nor do they talk clearly or directly enough about its performance values—the unspoken habits of thought and behavior built into the firm's definition of successful performance. After an initial employment period, many firms assume that cultural initiation is something that happens naturally and a bit mysteriously as a result of a normal process of socialization. (Christiansen and Stein, *Successful Onboarding*, pp. 64-65)

The irony of cultural norms is that they are often deductive and identified by what they *are not*, rather than what they are. Violations of norms are often the most visible demonstration of their existence in the first place. This is a painful way to experience culture. Leaders can help their new people avoid this pain by explaining culture within the team and organization and the norms that support them. Set the tone early and define your expectations. Culture is indeed brilliantly described as *the worst performance or behavior that you'll accept*. Outline what describes acceptable performance and behavior in your eyes, and you'll help the team and your new hire greatly.

So what aspects of culture should be described? Productivity, priorities, pace, and process are important. New hires need to know what work products, in terms of volume and quality, they're expected to provide. Certain roles require more exacting work than others, where the tolerance for mistakes may be very low. New hires need to know that so they can focus their attention on producing the standard expected. Likewise, while completing one "perfect" work product may be admirable, producing only one is unacceptable when five products of a certain quality were expected. This is where pace comes in—an understanding of the speed at which work activity should occur so new staff can match pace to meet expectations.

New people also need to understand what the priorities of their role are. This is a basic aspect of performance management, as all team members should know what their most important activities are at any given time. Lastly, they need to know process. While the teaching of process itself isn't a cultural matter, understanding whether the processes exist or not, where to find them, and why they exist help signal what the cultural priorities are. Organizations create and implement process around those operations they want to control outcomes for; so just as what gets measured gets done, what is structured gets monitored. This signals what's important to the organization.

Explaining norms around communication is important too. Is the communication culture formal or informal? Is it open and transparent, or is information shared more on a "need-to-know" basis? Are there preferences for formal memos and presentations or informal emails/discussions? Are group meetings structured and require preparation and information sent out in advance, or do they act as informal forums for idea-sharing and brainstorming? Which stakeholders require more formal communication, and which are informal in their style? Do team members need to use certain structures or "chains of command" for communication, conflict, and problem resolution?

It takes time to recover from serious cultural missteps, which can badly damage credibility. This is why new hires need your guidance to effectively navigate through culture as they establish themselves in the role. This will ultimately impact their productivity and engagement on the job. It requires a proactive approach from you, as you bear the primary responsibility for enculturation of your new people. It isn't an HR function and can't be accomplished in a two-hour orientation presentation on day one. It's going to take your time and engagement personally, as you are the one who builds and maintains culture on your team.

- *Do you describe the working culture and supporting norms within the organization and your team to your new hires?*
- *Do you discuss norms around important areas like productivity, pace, process, priorities, and communication to help new hires integrate well into the culture?*
- *Within the first two weeks of work do you have a clear and direct conversation with your new hires about your expectations for performance and behavior?*

INITIAL CAREER DEVELOPMENT AND SUPPORT

This is the aspect of onboarding we think about most commonly when new staff join. This support includes early training provided to new hires to familiarize them with systems, structures, and processes, as well as provide skill-based training specific to their jobs. As a leader, you need to actively engage in this process, but you can do so without being the primary deliverer of training. As a leader, you are ultimately responsible for effective early career development and support, but there are always other resources available to you for initial training.

Using mentoring, job shadowing, meetings with stakeholders, eLearning, formal classroom/webinar training, and other resources allows you to insert yourself into the process of early career development and support where you can have the most impact. It also shares the burden of day-to-day training and development in the early weeks of your new hire's career.

Match the format of training and development properly to the subject and you'll find that your new hire learns more effectively. Pettingell and Tobin remind us that "other competencies are better learned on the job than in the classroom. For example, developing a broad understanding of the organization's business is better learned by development activities such as assignment to a cross-functional team, job rotation, or an international assignment than by any classroom experience" (*The AMA Guide to Management Development*, p. 31).

Simple procedures and technical functions might be appropriately taught via eLearning, but interpersonal skills—such as leadership, sales, and customer service—and those requiring simulation and practice are better taught interactively. Adults learn best where they can both take in and apply knowledge quickly, and a lecture-based environment alone isn't very useful in that respect. Build in practice opportunities throughout the training process and you'll reinforce staff motivation when they see themselves successfully performing new skills.

To provide appropriate initial support, get to know your new hire early. This includes, during the first week, a conversation that helps define expectations around learning and growth. These may include questions like: What attracted you to the company and the role? What do you hope most to learn? What strengths do you believe you have? What areas of professional growth would you like to work on? What concerns you most about settling into your new role? What is the best way I can support your learning and growth, particularly during the first ninety days on the job? Do you have any long-term goals for career growth that we've not already discussed? Asking good questions and listening are important leadership traits that are particularly useful here. Your new team member wants to know that you're interested in their thoughts and feelings right from the very start and that you'll support their early career development and performance.

Harter and Wagner, in *12: The Elements of Great Managing*, point out that "for many people, it is progress that distinguishes a career from employment that is 'just a job.' Employees who have an opportunity to learn and grow at work are twice as likely as those on the other end of the scale to say they will spend their career with their company" (p. 173). Helping people quickly learn their roles and develop their skills fuels the motivation that personal growth builds and sustains.

New hires often complain about feeling overwhelmed by onboarding. It's natural for emotions to run higher during a time of significant change. This is often compounded when onboarding programs pack masses of learning into a tight window of time to quickly force productivity out of new people. In practice, the opposite often occurs, as information overload causes additional stress for learners. Reduced opportunities to retain information and practice new skills also occur. This approach is short-sighted, and pacing training—allowing for simulation, practice, and time to clarify information—is unlikely to increase overall time-to-productivity. It's also liable to result in higher sustained performance levels. Provide information in a logical, planned way and give what is necessary to do the job and place it in proper perspective within the organization. Don't swamp new team members with information that's irrelevant to their roles, or peripheral at best.

- *Do you use the variety of resources—such as eLearning, classroom training, mentors, job shadowing, and stakeholder meetings—to deliver early training/support for your new hire?*
- *Do you get to know your new hire as quickly as you can, including their own view on their strengths, areas for growth, and aspirations for learning and their careers?*
- *Do you pace the delivery of training or flood your new hires with as much information as possible to try to quickly make them productive in the role?*

THE FIRST WEEKS OF ONBOARDING

There are likely to be some subjects you'll want to cover in the first week or two, and others that can wait. Giving your new hire a tour of their worksite, including introductions to team members, helps make them feel more comfortable and welcome. If you've produced an onboarding schedule, then sit down on day one and explain it to your new team member. Talk about the plan for learning, and outline who the new hire will be meeting with (and the relevance of those people to the new hire's role). This decreases the stress that comes from uncertainty. Your new hire will be impressed with the fact that you've prepared well for their arrival and planned out their early experience.

Have the conversation about the operating environment early. New team members need an overview of the organization, its market position, the issues and environmental influences affecting company performance, and the strategy of your business unit and team. Everyone needs to be clear about the company's mission, vision, and purpose—and how their role supports them. Discuss your expectations for behavior and performance and go through the job description together.

Your new team member needs to understand how competence in their position contributes to the success of the team. Talk through the metrics used to assess their effectiveness in the role. If you do intend to use a mentor, make sure the introduction occurs within the first week or so. As the mentor will act as part of your new team member's support network, the earlier they get to know one another the better.

During the first several weeks, your new team member will likely participate in formal training sessions, job shadowing, self-learning and e-learning, meetings with stakeholders and their mentor, and periodic meetings with you as their leader. It's very important that you schedule regular time to meet on a one-on-one basis with your new hire. One of the biggest mistakes leaders make is to work hard to engage and convince a prospect to join their organization and then neglect regular, planned interactions with them over the crucial first few weeks.

Everything we do sends a signal to our people, and your new team member will be particularly sensitive to their environment and interactions. A lack of attention from you is going to go over badly, with your new hire feeling that he or she is far more engaged in their onboarding than you are. During the first couple of weeks, schedule time at least every other day or so to have a follow-up discussion so that you both can discuss progress and issues. You can move to having them less frequently as both you and your new hire's comfort level with progress increases. It's easier to reduce the cadence of meetings than to have to increase them, by which time your new team member is already struggling and the damage to their early engagement is already done.

- *How often do you meet with new hires during the first month of their employment?*
- *How well-organized is the schedule for the first two weeks of your new hire's experience?*
- *Do you explain right away how good performance in the new hire's role affects the success of the team and impacts others?*

ONGOING PEOPLE DEVELOPMENT ISSUES

Just as in life, where our early years are the most formative, so the early days of employment are for the integration and development of our team members. That's why we must place proper focus on onboarding. We can't forget that all team members deserve to be developed, however. This, of course, also depends upon their own effort, engagement, performance, and behavior, as these are the basic price of admission to the team and opportunity to remain on it. Those who are struggling need coaching and development to help them perform their roles. Those meeting expectations also deserve development; either to expand their skills and experience within their current positions, or prepare them for the next step in their careers if they desire promotion.

We all have a very basic human need to feel like we're making progress. It's part of the journey we equate with meaningfulness. Without a sense of personal and professional growth, our days become one repeating, monotonous cycle that gradually sap our energy and engagement. Just like businesses know that if they are not growing they're dying, we feel the same way emotionally when we're stagnant. Developing people feeds a business's heart and mind as well as its bottom line. Harter and Wagner, in *12: The Elements of Great Managing*, concluded the same: "Because each person is unique in her talents, strengths, situation, hopes, and personality, it is incumbent upon the employee and her manager to chart her future progress ... it is imperative they create that feeling of personal improvement. When employees feel they are learning and growing, they work harder and more efficiently" (p. 173).

The obvious message that development sends to our team members is that we value them, we believe in their potential to contribute further, and we're willing to invest resources into their professional growth. This naturally feels good, and our show of commitment is normally reciprocated with increased engagement and performance as the bond of loyalty strengthens.

As staff move from being novices to experienced performers, leaders sometimes neglect or deprioritize their development, particularly if they are "average" performers. These team members, who perform competently and can add value through their ideas and attitude, are sometimes overlooked in favor of those operating at the extremes (the "star" performer and the underperformer). Most team members are by definition "average," and there's nothing at all wrong with that. Performing fully satisfactorily should hold no shame, and we do well to remember that these people are the heart of a team and we shouldn't ignore their need for growth and progress. Our task is to raise the group's performance level over time so that the "average" performer's productivity increases. Move the entire bell curve to the right.

As a leader, think about developing your people in a planned, purposeful way, just like you did with your new hires. There's no reason to neglect the same level of planning for your people's development just because they moved out of the onboarding phase into that of an experienced practitioner.

Use the tools at your disposal to structure the development of your people and you'll see a dividend paid in terms of higher performance, engagement, and retention. What do you do today to purposefully plan for development? Do you discuss and document developmental goals? Do you use annual appraisal discussions and other regular one-on-one meetings to set and review these goals? Are they specific and include deadlines? Unless an individual development plan is documented, regularly discussed, and followed up on—just like any other achievement aim—then progress is unlikely to occur.

> ... to prepare individuals for promotion, the organization has an obligation to do more than merely identify and present future work requirements and performance. It must find some way to clarify— and to systematically close—the developmental gap between what possible successors can already do and what they must do to qualify for advancement. *Individual development planning* is the process of clarifying that developmental gap; internal development uses planned training, education, development, and other means— including on-the-job work assignments—to close developmental gaps and thereby meet succession needs. (Rothwell, *Effective Succession Planning*, p. 241)

Individual leaders are part of the larger process of succession planning in progressive firms that understand the importance of talent management. Even if your firm doesn't have a structure for succession management, as an individual leader you can effectively manage for professional growth and succession within your own team. Leaders who are good people developers leave a trail of happy careers behind them and are more likely to be noticed and promoted themselves.

Progressive leaders view intelligence as ever-developing and changing in people. They perceive themselves as a steward for knowledge rather than someone intellectually superior to the group. You aren't there to provide all the answers personally; you exist to use the knowledge and talent of the group to solve problems and make progress. If you believe you must always provide the answers and just direct the team to carry out your solutions then you are wasting a great deal of potential in your people, who will also notice it and go elsewhere to ensure their talent isn't squandered. Team members' potential is also wasted when their development becomes a chance undertaking. Don't let that be the fate of your people. Plan for it instead.

———————————————→

- *Do you train only to increase people's skills for the sake of short-term performance, or do you engage in long-term career development of your people?*
- *Do you plan for the growth and development of all your people, or only concentrate your attention on the underperformers and the "superstars"?*
- *Do you write down development plans for each of your people at least yearly, using performance appraisals or other tools— setting deadlines, and following up?*

←———————————————

IDENTIFY GAPS AND LEVERAGE TALENTS–COACH!

As we've discussed, identifying the innate strengths and areas of growth in people is a key leadership skill. It requires your engagement, sensitivity, and interest in others. Leaders who are transactional in their relationships will never truly awaken and leverage the potential in others. Such managers only work to take advantage of others' talents for their own immediate gain, seeking productivity as part of a bargain to be struck in the here and now. They never give something for nothing, nor do they expect their people to do so. Transactional leadership takes an unfortunately dim view of interpersonal relationships, seeing it as only within the context of a business contract. Such leaders use up and discard talent at an alarming rate.

This leadership tendency occurs more commonly than we'd like to admit. The transactional style is a philosophy that some might unfortunately believe in. It also occurs, however, because circumstances override the benign intent that leaders have for the welfare and development of their team members.

Sometimes the leader is on shaky ground and there's immediate pressure to perform, resources are scarce, or a need for results in the current financial period exists. The tendency is then to "panic buy" talent from the outside who might be able to "hit the ground running" (does this ever *really* occur?), or scramble to redeploy people based upon a largely superficial understanding of their talents and passion. Performance is never as good as it could be because of this, and the rollercoaster process of managing in a crisis isn't sustainable.

The best people developers mine for individual strengths to build upon and leverage. "Inspiring coaches see it as their purpose to look for the gold in their employees. Once these coaches find it, they coach their employees to refine that gold. They help their employees build better lives for themselves and others while producing winning results. In the crunch of daily demands, it is easy to forget a fundamental law of leadership: If your employees are successful, you are successful" (Colan and Davis-Colan, *The Power of Positive Coaching*, p. 41).

While many people believe they are adept at identifying their own strengths and weaknesses, that's rarely the case. Few people are highly self-aware and objective enough to seek and take feedback without filtering it through their own biases and emotions. Leaders who develop others help provide a more holistic perspective on strengths and areas for improvement so they can leverage brilliance and grow them more effectively.

Structuring learning for your individual team members doesn't have to be a complex process. Just add in a plan with some specifics and deadlines for development that will help both you and your people. You should engage regularly with team members in a way that helps counsel them. Relay suggestions to increase performance, and provide insight that helps others use talent in a way that results in personal growth. Any coach, in any of life's pursuits, will tell you that's the reason their role exists.

Coaching is by nature an ad hoc, on-demand activity that takes place whenever opportunities present themselves. There is a saying, however, that "Opportunity is where chance meets preparation." As leaders, we can't afford to be passengers on the coaching journey—we *are* the coach, after all. This means that we must look for opportunities to provide our people guidance. This doesn't happen without regular interaction with team members. It can happen from your office chair in video conferences, calls, or other discussions. And it certainly can happen when you are up walking around, personally speaking with your people face-to-face. Coaching is a saw sharpened through use. If you hope to perform as a leader and grow your own expertise, you have to learn to develop others. Coaching expertise isn't something that people either magically have or don't have. No one is born a great coach, no more than they are born a great leader.

- ***Do you view every interaction with others at work only as a business transaction struck between two people who exchange something of worth?***
- ***Do you invest in others without expectation of immediate (if ever) return, or are you only interested in others who have something of value you can immediately use?***
- ***Are you proactive in your approach to communicating and connecting with others, and regularly take up opportunities to practice and refine your coaching skills?***

USE THE DEVELOPMENT
RESOURCES AT YOUR DISPOSAL

Use the variety of people development resources that are available, even if your organization doesn't have a learning and development function or a formal succession planning structure. As the leader, your role in the development of your people is always primary. With a little forethought, you can use work experiences to grow your team members without having it dominate your time personally.

"Job enrichment" is one means of doing just that. Job enrichment entails your people being asked to perform their role to a higher standard than in the past, or to take lead responsibility for initiatives that they have only participated in previously. Asking people to take end-to-end ownership of an initiative allows them to see how activities integrate together to result in group performance. This provides greater meaning to workplace activity through an understanding of how individual performance contributes to company success. Asking people to analyze a situation or data and make recommendations for action is also a part of job enrichment.

Job enrichment is about people going deeper into their roles to gain thorough expertise. Opportunities abound for you to enrich others' jobs. It requires you to give up some authority and control to allow others the latitude to develop more quickly. This doesn't mean letting them flounder or fail on a large initiative; it merely means you're stepping back into the shadows and allowing your people to shine, stepping in only to steer them away from the rocky shores of large, expensive, or repeated errors.

As Liz Wiseman said in *Multipliers*, "try supersizing someone's job. Assess their current capabilities and give them a challenge that is a size too big. Give an individual contributor a leadership role; give a first-line manager more decision-making power. If they seem startled, acknowledge that the role or responsibility might feel awkward at first. Then step back and watch them grow into it" (p. 60).

"Job enlargement" is a different method of experiential learning and development. This is where you ask your people to take on new skills and operate outside of their area of traditional expertise. You make the job wider rather than deeper by asking a team member to take responsibility for an initiative that includes activities they haven't experienced before. It may be one that requires them to work with new people, technology, or information— for example, asking an IT support practitioner to take responsibility for an initiative that also involves user acceptance testing activities that they haven't experienced before. Likewise, asking a learning and development practitioner to be involved with the selection of individuals entering into the company's graduate employment or internship programs demonstrates job enlargement.

The opportunity to lead a project or initiative, whether it constitutes job enrichment/enlargement or not, allows your people to hone their own coaching, leadership, influencing, problem resolution, resource coordination, and planning skills. Individuals carry such skills, practiced and grown, throughout their careers. Taking charge of a project and seeing an initiative through from beginning to end can be an invaluable learning experience.

You can also develop your people through offering interim assignments and job rotation. This might be for a set period of time, once a project is complete, or until your team member reaches a certain performance level that allows them to move onto the next phase in their career development. These assignments have an anticipated end date. This is the main difference between them and a lateral career move, which is a conscious career move into another role of similar level rather than one that acts as a typical promotion. Exposure to different business areas and broadening of expertise provide a more holistic perspective of the business, and are reasons staff members and leaders may choose lateral movement. It's a means of personal and professional growth that can, in the longer term, pay a dividend in terms of promotability.

Whatever the means of learning through experience, it helps people to connect professional growth to the organization's strategy and operating success. This is a necessity and a real advantage. "Focusing on individual development apart from organizational strategy is simply providing competitors and headhunters with better people for recruitment. Action learning, designed to address key organizational challenges can often provide solutions just as insightful and pragmatic as can outside consultants and it also contributes to the development of both the individual and the organization" (Bleak and Fulmer, *The Leadership Advantage*, p. 29).

Whether a formal, structured mentoring program exists or not, anyone in need of additional support for their growth and performance can benefit from having the right mentor. Many successful leaders, in fact, credit their professional growth to having at least one impactful mentor during their careers. We all are experts at something, and each of us has an opportunity to grow in some area.

As long as we represent ourselves and our organization in a professional, positive manner and show a willingness to communicate and invest in others, we have the potential to mentor during our careers. Students gain an additional perspective on an issue or subject from an experienced employee outside of their own manager; someone who can provide a practical, hands-on view of the issue.

For the mentor, benefits abound also. You can facilitate a pairing between coworkers to use the resources within the organization more effectively. In addition, you can use individuals who are experts in certain areas to educate team members in group meetings. This allows them to educate and coach the group on an ad hoc basis in order to share best practice and increase collective skill. This often feels good for the "expert" who is allowed to showcase their knowledge and build their presentation and coaching skills, while also being an efficient use of time to train the group.

Part of your role in developing others is also to get feedback to them—your own, as well as others'. Hopefully you have regular one-on-one discussions with your people, which includes time for each of you to give and receive feedback and discuss development opportunities. These conversations help your people see that feedback is a highly valuable resource to mold behavior and performance and help them grow professionally. Feedback then becomes a normal part of the work experience, not something to be approached with trepidation. Encourage your people to also seek feedback from other stakeholders in order to provide a well-rounded picture of how they're perceived within the organization.

If you do not already have a broad 360-degree view of your people prior to annual appraisal discussions, you should seek feedback as good practice. Encourage your people to also use 360-degree feedback tools if they exist within your organization to facilitate information gathering and analysis. Little will increase career development further and faster than a steady flow of meaningful feedback—together with the willingness to accept and make adjustments based upon it.

- *Do you have a mentor of your own to help accelerate your growth as a leader?*
- *Do you use job enrichment, job enlargement, project participation, and job rotation to develop your people via workplace experiences?*
- *Do you facilitate feedback gathering, including 360-degree feedback where possible, to help your people better understand how others perceive their performance/behavior?*

SUCCESSION PLANNING

Within many teams, there are roles seen as the next logical step in a career path for your people. It may be a higher-level role within the same discipline or another position with greater responsibility, authority, and impact. If these exist on your team, consider planning for succession as good leadership practice, particularly if you operate in middle or senior management where numbers of your direct reports may be leaders themselves. If you're effective in leadership development yourself and perform well in your role, then you also increase your own chances of promotion by having a ready-made replacement for your current leadership position.

We know that "jobs for life" exist only in theory. It's increasingly rare that individuals stay in one company, let alone one position, during their entire careers. Many people, even if they want to stay within your organization, will want to challenge themselves in a new role over time. This may or may not be a role on your team. Direct reports become peers and people transfer across locations and business units, so the concept of being a steward for talent is intimately connected to people development.

If you can promote people into progressively more complex, impactful, and hard-to-fill roles—backfilling the vacated positions with others internally in turn (or externally as needed)—then you have the potential to progress multiple careers in a conveyor belt of talent development. This retains proprietary knowledge and continues to engage your people. As long as appropriate internal candidates are chosen, time-to-productivity is likely to decrease and overall productivity increase because culture, systems, processes, and other nuances within the organization are already known to them. All that's left is for them to become proficient in their new job duties and responsibilities. On a macrolevel, succession planning is also an increasing concern in organizations generally:

> Succession planning is needed for several reasons. One key reason is that the current workforce is aging rapidly ... Not only do organizations need to prepare for a mass exodus of older workers, they must prepare for life with fewer workers in general. Furthermore, many baby boomer executives have the talents and capabilities that many high-potential and emerging leaders do not yet possess. If these talents are not transferred effectively to younger leaders and future leaders, they will become lost forever. One thing is sure: The retention of key talent for every organization is no longer a nice-to-have. (Mattone, *Talent Leadership*, p. 108)

In workplaces pushing for continual improvement and increasing efficiency, leaders don't have the luxury of allowing chairs to remain empty for extended periods. When the ability to promote staff upward in the organization exists instead, then risk is also being managed. This is because external backfills then occur in lower-level positions where the pool of talent is more plentiful and the consequences of getting the hiring decision "wrong" is lessened.

The failure to manage talent effectively also causes a shortage of leadership pools that prevents organizations from expanding and executing on their strategic goals. This includes succession planning and people development to prevent hiring people into positions they are less-than-well-qualified for. The impact of making such compromises with hiring can be particularly devastating to the organization in the longer term.

Succession planning shouldn't be focused solely on leadership positions. Many specialist and hard-to-recruit roles are wise to plan succession for. This is common in information technology, finance, human resources, and other disciplines. Knowing who may be able to step up internally when the next senior accountant, network architect, human resource generalist, or other specialist role comes open will help your team maintain productivity and continuity, keep knowledge within the group, and retain your people. The general benefits of succession planning are universal, regardless of the type of role.

Your organization might have some formal succession planning and management process that can help you. If none exists, you can still use some very simple methods and tools to plan for succession and focus your development efforts to close skills gaps. The 9-box process is likely the best known, which is nothing more than a 3-by-3 grid with "current performance" on one axis and "future potential" on the other. By assessing where your people lie on the grid, you can better define your approach to managing and developing talent within your team.

People who are performing adequately or well and have medium to high potential are more likely to be future succession candidates. Team members who perform adequately to well and have low potential to move beyond their roles might be approached to build experience and expand the scope of responsibility within their current positions. Individuals who are struggling to perform (even if they have higher potential) need to be coached up or be removed from the team if their underperformance can't be successfully addressed.

A second 9-box grid with "risk of loss" on one axis and "impact of loss" on the other is also useful when assessing team members. Looking at the impact of loss of individual team members creates urgency and helps prioritize addressing development and retention for them, particularly if their risk and impact of loss is anything other than low. We all have finite resources and choices to make in using them—this includes our own time, effort, and attention as leaders. Everyone deserves an opportunity to grow themselves and their careers, but the price of dedicating the organization's precious resources is today's performance. How, and how much, resources are dedicated to individuals will also depend on the view of their future potential.

The reality is that not everyone will be treated exactly the same when you plan for succession and manage talent, and that's okay. Individual team members will vary in terms of their performance level, the intangibles they bring to the team, and their future potential to contribute to the organization. Organizations regularly make choices about where to dedicate their effort and resources to achieve the greatest success. This happens when businesses make decisions to invest in certain markets, capital resources, products, and services. Resources are not spread evenly across these facets of operations, and neither are they with our people. You have to make choices about where you see the greatest chances of contribution and success via the people you are entrusted to guide. As long as you understand that people change and grow, and that your assessment of them using tools such as 9-box is only a point-in-time view, you can shift resources from time to time as your outlook on team members changes.

- *Do you plan for succession on your team, using formal processes or methods such as 9-box to help assess your talent?*
- *Do you consciously look at your internal talent when openings first arise so that you can identify and speak to internal candidates to help promote and fill jobs with qualified people?*
- *Do you use succession planning for only leadership positions/talent, or do you extend this to other positions on your team or in your organization?*

DEVELOPING LEADERS

While we discussed the need to develop all our staff, growing current and future leaders remains a priority because of the impact of those occupying such roles. Leaders play such a pivotal part in helping organizations perform and determine how fulfilling the work experience is for team members. Because of this, as a leader you're also tasked with helping produce more leaders—particularly if you're in a middle or upper management role where you lead those who lead others. As your position level increases, so does your potential to impact the organization through your leadership development efforts. The profound effect of leadership upon the fate of companies is undeniable.

Leadership isn't a subject that is covered meaningfully in education settings at the undergraduate level, leaving it to be developed almost exclusively on the job. When individuals make their first career move into management, it's often without the benefit of having been through prior leadership development on the job. This typically leaves those first-line supervisors, who are closest to the customer and the face of the organization to most staff, learning how to lead only once they're in the role. Whether your organization has a formal program or not, as a leader you can build leadership learning into the development plans you have for your current and potential managers.

The Leadership Core is all about building your capabilities to manage others, and hopefully some of the issues we've discussed resonate with you and you can use them to help develop others. In preparing individuals to supervise, management skills (management reporting, scheduling, budgeting, allocating resources, mitigating risk, etc.) are often emphasized. These are indeed important skills to help achieve the goals set for leaders and their teams. Very real issues must be addressed in order to operationalize strategies.

Leadership competencies, including those we've reviewed in this book, are the other half of needed expertise. *Management* often focuses on control over things (money, time, plans, resources, risk, etc.). *Leadership* focuses on people—how individual and collective talents are utilized to gain results—and it focuses on supporting staff in alignment with organizational aims. It's key to remember both aspects—*leadership* and *management*—to prepare others properly to take on supervisory roles. Remember that you need to capture hearts *and* minds to get hands and feet moving in the direction of success.

Make sure that the development of leaders aligns with business strategy; skills, competencies, and learning experiences need to support the direction of the business and its strategic aims. By asking yourself how the development activities you assign to your people align with strategy, you can ensure that you build a pool of leadership talent that has continued relevance.

Accountability remains a cornerstone of execution at work and life, which we've talked about at length already. Follow up to ensure that learning activities are completed well and timely, that staff did indeed gain knowledge and applied it in practice, and that learning resulted in improved performance. You don't have to undertake all these activities on your own, as you may have training professionals, management colleagues, and others who can support you. You do, however, bear the ultimate responsibility for making good follow-up happen as you develop people.

If you occupy a higher management role, then hold your own leadership subordinates responsible for development of their own people by following up with them, in turn. This is the "chain of accountability" which is sometimes weak in organizations, where leaders aren't held sufficiently responsible for the primary leadership activities they should be undertaking. Are your leaders assessed on employee turnover, including early turnover? How about employee engagement, including the outcomes of engagement surveys and the execution of follow-up plans to address areas of weakness? What about internal promotion rates? Productivity per FTE, revenue per FTE, and group performance metrics? Is the average number of voluntary training courses attended per FTE tracked? What about the percentage of performance appraisals delivered on time? You can choose from lots of metrics to assess leadership effectiveness.

When persistent problems with team morale, engagement, performance, and efficiency exist, you have a leadership problem not a followership issue. Accountability is primarily a top-down affair within organizations. When executives and senior managers don't hold other leadership levels accountable for results—which are accomplished by and through team members—then a weak performance culture exists. This includes people development activity. If no one follows up to ensure that development plans are created and executed, that learning initiatives are undertaken and the organization is improved as a result, then results in this area largely come down to individual employees taking initiative on their own to learn. That is not a recipe for success. People learn when they both want to and are held accountable for learning, and it's best that self-accountability isn't the sole strategy here.

- *Do you identify potential and develop plans to prepare team members for future leadership roles?*
- *If you are a senior leader, do you hold your leadership subordinates truly accountable for staff performance, development, retention, and engagement?*

SOME FINAL THOUGHTS

If you've achieved a leadership position or aspire to one, and have a true interest in helping others succeed, then congratulations. It sounds like you've found a role that matches your career interests well. You're also in a role that has the potential to profoundly influence the organization and its people. In fact, for your team members you *are* the organization, or at least its face. They form their opinions of how organized, professional, supportive, prestigious, and ambitious their workplace is primarily through their interactions with *you*. Others may leave their impressions too, but individuals' perspectives of whether they work in a fulfilling job with an opportunity to succeed and grow will be molded mainly by you. This is a reality Lee J. Colan also explained, stating that "our world of work is influenced by our direct leader. If I work in a crummy place but my boss is terrific, then I feel good about work and give everything I have to my team. On the contrary, I might work for a world-class organization, but my boss is not so hot. As hard as I might try, it becomes very difficult for me to give 110 percent to the team. Bottom line: We work for people, not companies … and employees generally leave people, not companies" (*Engaging the Hearts and Minds of All Your Employees*, p. 25).

This is the reality of work. We work with people—and it's people, not companies, that shape our view of our career choices. There are no prizes for brilliance alone in leadership. Plenty of smart people, some already in leadership roles, don't comprehend that you cannot order loyalty, engagement, and discretionary effort. It takes much more than data and logic to drive people down the road where the extra mile lies because that's an emotional journey. The grandest of plans just don't come to pass without connecting, coaching, and inspiring—and that is about what's in your heart, not your head.

Hopefully you have picked up a greater appreciation of this reality as we've discussed the leadership competencies necessary for success. There's no one magic leadership formula, however, and you will take away different perspectives on leadership based on where you are on your journey. The skeptics will often point to the "people first" perspective on leadership as naïve, idealistic, and out of touch with the needs of today's work environments. They say that you get to choose either "people first" or performance, but you can't have both. I don't believe that and think when people are placed as a priority, good performance naturally follows—as long as leadership is competent and effective. The benefit for you and the organization? An engine for sustainable, repeatable performance is built for the long term.

I once watched a very entertaining and informative TED Talk by Jason Clarke on "Embracing Change." In it, he mentioned that if you're young today, your career is about destiny; if you're older, it's about legacy. I think if you are a leader your destiny *is* to leave a legacy—a positive one where organizations you've worked within and people you touched are better off because you were there. We all leave a legacy. As a leader, you control what that is by feeling the weight of your position and taking responsibility for being a constructive resource for others. When others remember working with you as their leader, they then will do so fondly and with a smile.

ABOUT THE AUTHOR

William Schirmer is a senior management professional in Human Resources, having been involved with HR, Talent Management, and Learning & Development functions for domestic and international firms over more than twenty years. His expertise includes the creation and deployment of leadership development programs for a number of organizations. William holds USA, UK, and Global Human Resource certifications. His undergraduate study in Political & Behavioral Sciences was completed via Minnesota State University-Mankato in the USA. William completed his Graduate Degrees in Human Resource Management via Fort Hays State University in the USA and Social Sciences via the University of Leicester in the United Kingdom. William grew up in Minnesota and is a lover of the outdoors, travel, motorcycling, and exercise. He's a proud father of three grown children: Daniel, Richard, and Alyssa.

BIBLIOGRAPHY

Abrashoff, Michael. *It's Your Ship*. New York: Business Plus, 2002.

Banks, Lydia. *Motivation in the Workplace*. USA: American Media Publishing, 1997.

Blanchard, Ken. *The Heart of a Leader*. Colorado Springs, USA: David C. Cook, 2007.

Bleak, Jared and Robert Fulmer. *The Leadership Advantage*. New York: American Management Association, 2008.

Bossidy, Larry and Ram Charan. *Execution: The Discipline of Getting Things Done*. New York: Crown Business, 2002.

Bridges, Susan and William Bridges. *Managing Transitions: Making the Most of Change*. London: Nicholas Brealey Publishing, 2017.

Buckingham, Marcus. *The One Thing You Need to Know*. New York: Free Press, 2005.

Cameron, Esther and Mike Green. *Making Sense of Change Management*. London: Kogan Page, 2004.

Cashman, Kevin. *Leadership from the Inside Out*. Provo, Utah, USA: Executive Excellence Publishing, 1998.

Chapman, Gary and Paul White. *The 5 Languages of Appreciation in the Workplace*. Chicago: Northfield Publishing, 2011.

Charan, Ram and Bill Conaty. *The Talent Masters*. New York: Crown Business, 2010.

Christiansen, Lilith and Mark Stein. *Successful Onboarding*. New York: McGraw Hill, 2010.

Colan, Lee. *Engaging the Hearts and Minds of All Your Employees*. New York: McGraw Hill, 2009.

Colan, Lee and Julie Davis-Colan. *The Power of Positive Coaching*. New York: McGraw Hill, 2019.

Connors, Roger, Craig Hickman, and Tom Smith. *The Oz Principle*. New York: Portfolio, 2004.

Cottrell, David. *Monday Morning Choices: 12 Powerful Ways to Go from Everyday to Extraordinary*. New York: Collins, 2008.

Cottrell, David. *Monday Morning Motivation*. New York: Harper Business, 2009.

Grenny, Joseph, Ron McMillan, Kerry Patterson, and Al Switzler. *Crucial Conversations*. New York: McGraw-Hill, 2002.

Drollet, Bonita and Thomas Harvey. *Building Teams, Building People*. New York: Rowman & Littlefield Education, 2005.

Evans, Henry. *Winning with Accountability*. USA: Cornerstone Leadership Institute, 2008.

Fowler, Susan. *Why Motivating People Doesn't Work ... and What Does*. San Francisco: Berrett-Koehler, 2004.

George, Bill. *Discover Your True North*. New Jersey, USA: John Wiley & Sons Inc., 2015.

Gilley, Jerry and Ann Maycunich. *Organizational Learning Performance and Change*. Cambridge, Mass., USA: Perseus Publishing, 2000.

Grant, Adam. *Give and Take*. New York: Penguin Books, 2013.

Harpelund, Christian, Morten Hojberg, and Kasper Ulf Nielsen. *Onboarding: Getting New Hires Off to a Flying Start.* United Kingdom: Emerald Publishing, 2019.

Harter, James and Rodd Wagner. *12: The Elements of Great Managing.* New York: Gallup Press, 2006.

Harvard Business Press. *Managing Change and Transition.* Boston: Harvard Business School Publishing Corporation, 2003.

Harvard Business Review. "Building Better Teams." Boston: Harvard Business Review Press, 2011.

Harvard Business Review. "On Change Management." Boston: Harvard Business Review Press, 2011.

Heath, Chip and Dan Heath. *Switch: How to Change Things When Change Is Hard.* New York: Random House, 2010.

Hiam, Alexander. *Motivational Management.* New York: American Management Association, 2003.

Hodges, Julie. *Managing and Leading People through Organizational Change.* London: Kogan Page, 2016.

Holiday, Ryan. *Ego Is the Enemy.* New York: Portfolio/Penguin, 2016.

Hunter, James. *The World's Most Powerful Leadership Principle: How to Become a Servant Leader.* New York: Crown Business, 2004.

King, David, Ranjit Sidhu, Dan Skelsey, and Richard Smith. *The Effective Change Manager's Handbook.* London: Kogan Page, 2015.

Kotter, John. *Leading Change.* Boston: Harvard Business School Press, 1996.

Kouzes, James and Barry Posner. *A Leader's Legacy.* San Francisco: Jossey-Bass, 2006.

Marciano, Paul L. *Carrots and Sticks Don't Work.* New York: McGraw Hill, 2010.

Mattone, John. *Talent Leadership*. New York: American Management Association, 2013.

Maxwell, John. *Developing the Leaders around You*. Nashville, USA: Thomas Nelson Publishers, 1995.

Maxwell, John. *Encouragement Changes Everything*. Nashville, USA: Nelson Business, 2008.

Novak, David. *Taking People with You*. New York: Portfolio/Penguin, 2012.

Pausch, Randy. *The Last Lecture (Video)*. USA: Disney Educational Publications.

Petro, Rich and Art Petty. *Practical Lessons in Leadership*. Victoria, BC, Canada: Trafford Publishing, 2007.

Pettingell, Margaret and Daniel Tobin. *The AMA Guide to Management Development*. New York: American Management Association, 2008.

Rothwell, William. *Effective Succession Planning*. New York: American Management Association, 2010.

Sanborn, Mark. *The Fred Factor*. New York: Currency/Doubleday, 2004.

Sinek, Simon. *Leaders Eat Last*. New York: Portfolio/Penguin, 2014

Thomas, Kenneth. *Intrinsic Motivation at Work*. San Francisco: Berrett-Koehler, 2000.

Watkins, Michael. *The First 90 Days*. Boston: Harvard Business Review Press, 2013.

Whitney, Diana, *Appreciative Leadership*. New York: McGraw Hill, 2010.

Wiseman, Liz. *Multipliers*. USA: Harper Business, 2017.

A free ebook edition is available with the purchase of this book.

To claim your free ebook edition:

1. Visit MorganJamesBOGO.com
2. Sign your name CLEARLY in the space
3. Complete the form and submit a photo of the entire copyright page
4. You or your friend can download the ebook to your preferred device

Morgan James BOGO™

A **FREE** ebook edition is available for you or a friend with the purchase of this print book.

CLEARLY SIGN YOUR NAME ABOVE

Instructions to claim your free ebook edition:
1. Visit MorganJamesBOGO.com
2. Sign your name CLEARLY in the space above
3. Complete the form and submit a photo of this entire page
4. You or your friend can download the ebook to your preferred device

Print & Digital Together Forever.

Snap a photo   Free ebook   Read anywhere

Printed in the USA
CPSIA information can be obtained
at www.ICGtesting.com
JSHW022215140824
68134JS00018B/1060